I0101961

# THE SHAKING

# &

# THE GLORY

## DR. TUNDE BOLANTA

*The Shaking and The Glory*

Restoration Bible Church and Ministries

©Tunde Bolanta

Published in 2020

by

Winning Faith Publications

London. England

ISBN: 978-1-907095-39-9

For copyrights usage or more copies, write to:

The Publication Department,

Restoration Bible Church & Ministries, Inc., P. O. Box 1485, Kaduna, Nigeria.

# TABLE OF CONTENT

# APPRECIATION

I wish to convey my profound gratitude to our ministry friends and partners in the United Kingdom who have graciously released this book THE SHAKING AND THE GLORY on Amazon globally. May the Lord cause His face to shine upon you and give you rest on every side.

Likewise, I am very grateful for the tireless and diligent work of our editorial team in Nigeria. Your labour of love shall be rewarded. I am indebted to my wife, Pastor Tina for her prayerful support and input and editorial work on this book. You are truly a help meet made in heaven.

My greatest appreciation goes to the Almighty God for His inspiration and enablement, I pray that this book will help prepare the church for the harvest and the catching away of the church.

# FOREWORD

Global events of the last days are a departure from what is normal, places in the world that have been relatively quiet from evil attacks are suddenly in the eye of the storm.

The world is experiencing more shaking such as terror attacks, disasters, communal violence, pandemics, racism, higher crime rates, ethnic and religious cleansing and a general surge of evil attacks, things came to a head globally with the COVID 19 pandemic, which brought about a global lock down.

The book THE SHAKING AND THE GLORY is focused on giving the believer a scriptural perspective on the purpose of God for the church when shaking occurs. In the book of Hebrews, God promised to shake everything that can be shaken. This is indicative of a season of sifting when chaff is removed from wheat. When God came down on Mount Sinai, there was a lot of shaking but his goal was to become intimate with Israel and put his fear in them but they would not come close to him in personal intimacy.

They preferred to hear from Moses rather than God. Personal intimacy is one of the goals of heaven when there is a shaking.

The season of shaking is a time when God allows anything not built on him to be removed in the lives of believers and the church. It is a time of training and raising of an elite army. God is not the author of disease and chaos but he recreates something good from it.

In the book of Genesis chapter one, there was darkness on the face of the deep but

God's Spirit was moving to recreate something good out of the darkness. It is a time of training. The Lord Jesus went through the wilderness as other leaders such as Moses, Elijah and Paul. Such seasons of shaking in the wilderness is for personal growth and revelation. The season of separation represents a boot camp for the believer. God wants an elite army for the last days and the season of shaking is part of the preparation of God's army.

The time of shaking as you would have when an aircraft goes into violent turbulence is a time people re-examine what is really important to them, they may say their best prayers and promise to be better persons. God expects the believer to re-examine his life and consecrate his life in a new way.

A life that is not surrendered or in a backslidden state cannot reap the great harvest. A church that is focused on self and the mundane cannot reap the great harvest in the face of renewed and increased aggression from Hell. One of the goal of God's shaking is to press the reset button and have a house cleaning in the life of the church.

There must be repentance in the altar and the pews. Those whose consciences have become seared, those who have backslidden but are going through the motions are being given an opportunity to repent and reconsider their ways in a season of shaking. It is also a time when God exposes false ministers and brethren.

When there is a storm, hidden things are revealed by the violence of the wind. God is bringing the church into a season of spiritual awakening and she cannot go into it encumbered. The believers must be equipped using the whole armor of God to soar as eagles overcoming the storms and reaping the end time harvest.

As the end of the age beckons, the church must not be allergic to persecution, the early church were battle hardened as they allowed the Holy Spirit to prepare them. The whole creation is groaning like a woman in labour, the devil will throw up more challenges because his time is short.

Believers must be ready to make sacrifices in order to reap the great harvest of souls in the last days. The church of the first century regarded it as an honour to suffer for the Lord. The world will become more intolerant of the church and believers will need to stand up and contend for their faith.

Although many believers on the frontlines have paid the supreme price for their faith; others believers elsewhere will find persecution to be more subtle whereby they are persecuted because of foundational beliefs of their faith. Faith that costs nothing means nothing.

As the body of Christ, we need to be reminded that Jesus told us the world will hate us on his account. As pressure mounts, we must be more interested in representing Jesus well; we must be focused on sacrificing our comfort for our convictions.

I pray that the Holy Spirit will multiply grace to the church as we prepare for a great awakening and world harvest of the last days.

DR TUNDE BOLANTA

# ENDORSEMENTS

I hear so many people today crying out for answers. "What is happening around us? Is this the end of the world? What is God saying?" People are desperate for a word from God in this season. I am so thankful that God raised up a seasoned prophetic voice in Nigeria.

I have known and respected Rev. Tunde Bolanta for many years, so I was not surprised when he went in his prayer closet in early 2020 and came out with a message like the one found in this book, THE SHAKING AND THE GLORY.

The book confirms so much of what I have sensed myself during the coronavirus

pandemic that began in March. It will be
through a time of shaking and spiritual
warfare that the church will be prepared for
the greatest harvest season in history. If you
are finding yourself weary from the struggle
of 2020, you will find hope and comfort in
this book. Read it and prepare for a global
spiritual awakening.

**J. LEE GRADY**
*Former Editor, Charisma Magazine*
*Director, The Mordecai Project*


Once again, my highly esteemed friend,
Apostle Tunde Bolanta, has written a book
that is a direct message from the heart of
God to the Church. During these uncertain
and remarkably challenging times around
the globe, so many within the Church have
questions.

We have had a proliferation of "prophets"
who have made their livings telling folks

what they want to hear. Yet, Apostle Tunde, in THE SHAKING AND THE GLORY, is telling the Church what they must hear in order to remain strong for the great harvest of souls just ahead.

Although it contains prophetic messages, this book has strong teaching that will help individuals prepare to be effective, productive, End-Time warriors. This is one that will be an ongoing instructional manual, so keep it in plain sight.

You will want to reference it time and time again, as you continue to strengthen yourself through the shaking— so that you can enjoy all the glory to come!

**DONNA J. SCHAMBACH,**
*President and CEO*
*SCHAMBACH MINISTRIES*
*INTERNATIONAL*
*Tyler, Texas USA*

Apostle Tunde Bolanta lives in a shaken place. It's not shaken by a passing pandemic or economic hardship. But it's shaken by the glory of the Lord that brings down strongholds of terror, violence, deception and witchcraft.

He's learned to make his bed in hell. He sits at the table prepared by God in the presence of enemies. And though he "walks through the valley of the shadow of death", he is not afraid because he's saturated in the glory of the Lord.

I know the honor of standing in his pulpit and experiencing the Shekinah of God in that glorious House of thousands. Tunde Bolanta is a set man in his beloved Nigeria, and a sent man to the uttermost parts of the earth.

**BISHOP PAUL FRANCIS LANIER**
*Founder, Hope Community Church. Winston-Salem, North Carolina USA*

There is little question that we are living in a season where the world is shaking. The everyday flow of life as we have known it has been disrupted globally. God is never without a plan and a purpose, and His people should not be either! I know of few people who hear the voice of the Lord as clearly as my good friend and brother, Bishop, Dr. Tunde Bolanta.

This Book is no exception to that reality. It is a clear word of instruction from Heaven for the days we are living in. I strongly recommend this book to every Believer in Jesus in this hour, and wish it could be the marching orders for every church!

Don't merely read it. Study it and ask, 'What is my part to do and become?' You will be blessed in the journey!

**PASTOR JEFF TARBOX**
*Founding Pastor*
*New Life Church Maine*

It was Ralph Waldo Emerson who once said, "People wish to be settled; only as far as they are unsettled is there any hope for them." If I were to rephrase this statement in the light of the title of this book, it would read: "People want the glory of God; but only as far as they are willing to go through the shaking process will they manifest His glory."

There is no denying the fact that the world has experienced the worst kinds of chaos and upheaval in recent times. The natural way of looking at these things is from the untold hardships and sufferings they bring about. Another way however is from the perspective of God's shaking, preparing His children for His glory. That, precisely, is the crux of this book.

I have known the author, Dr Tunde Bolanta, for decades and he has been consistent as a preacher and teacher of the Word. His passion for a church without blemish—a church fully equipped to fulfil her divine mandate, particularly in these end-times — is unfeigned.

In 'The Shaking & the Glory', he is emphatic that God is raising an end-time army. He explores the tools and weapons needed by that army to accomplish God's purpose and gives biblical insights on how to acquire them. Although his style is hard-hitting, the book is pleasantly solution-centred.

Dr Bolanta is not one who will dance around a problem: he says it as it is. And that runs through every chapter of this book. If you desire to be a part of God's end-time victorious army, this is one book you must read.

**TAIWO ODUKOYA**
*Senior Pastor,*
*The Fountain of Life Church*
*Ilupeju, Lagos*
*Nigeria*

"THE SHAKING & THE GLORY" is a very timely book written and released to the Body of Christ, especially during the current global Corona pandemic which took virtually the whole world, including most Christians by surprise.

The author of this book is a proven and time-tested prophetic-apostle whose kingdom-labors and exploits have taken him to many nations and Christian denominations. This easy-to-read book is well-written and contains strong prophetic utterances, admonitions and warnings, as well as messages of comfort and reassurance for God's people.

Through this book, Dr. Tunde Bolanta, like Gideon of old, is blowing the trumpet and calling for serious Christians who will enlist in the spiritual army that God is building for His end times kingdom-agenda for the world and especially for His Church. Thank you, my dear brother and special friend, for faithfully delivering what the Spirit is currently saying to the churches (Rev.2:17). Your service to the saints will help prepare the Church for her Finest Hour!... Maranatha!... Shalom!

**REV.JOHN OKPOSIO MARSHAL,**

*President, NewBreed Revival Ministries, Port-Harcourt, Nigeria.*

Rev. Dr. Tunde Bolanta is a refreshing and delightful carrier of the presence and purpose of God to his generation. He is truly a prophetic voice with a clarion call to Godliness.

Global pandemic? New normal? This book gives us God's perspective. Straight-forward, biblically sound, and filled with helpful application; Dr. Bolanta gives us a manual for overcoming during this crisis.

**BISHOP HAROLD PRESLEY**
*Regional Director IPHC in NW Europe*

There is surely a shaking in this unprecedented hour. Everything not tethered to the Altar will sink like shifting sand. This shaking requires much from the Remnant. As Pastor Tunde's life and ministry so personally display, "Faith that cost you nothing means nothing."

Reading these prophetic utterances from a man who knows first-hand the fire of persecution ignites a hunger in our souls to take our place in this spiritual war. Pastor Tunde evokes a clarion call to believers who move with the full armour of God. The world has never needed us more. May we ingest this equipping Pastor Tunde offers through God's Word in such a way that the world around us wants what we possess.

For those battle-ready warriors ready to arise from their slumber, exercise the authority and power Jesus died to give us, and turn this world upside down for the Glory of God's Great Name . . . for THOSE, this book is essential! The battle will be intense but the victory is already won!

**DR. DEBBIE LANIER**
*Co-Founder,*
*Hope Community Church. Winston-Salem,*
*North Carolina USA*

I have thoroughly enjoyed reading "THE SHAKING AND THE GLORY" by Dr. Tunde Bolanta. Shaking seasons are permitted by heaven not to break believers, but to turn them into the valiant child of God that they were destined to be.

In this marvellous book, Dr. Tunde Bolanta draws from his rich knowledge of the holy scriptures coupled with testimonies borne out of decades of practical experience as a result of living and ministering in the frontlines of gospel ministry. He shares through this excellently written book, his deep understanding of God's realms of glory, and how to effectively navigate the different seasons of God's dealings.

This book is a must-read for any child of God who wants to learn to become a victorious soldier in the Lord's army; the insights on the armour of God will show you how. You will become a prayer champion by learning from the author how to pray, using the different manner of prayers revealed in the scriptures.

Are you hungry for more of God? Are you willing to be numbered by heaven amongst God's elite force? Have you always wondered how you can be a battle-hardened, unconquerable, effective, unstoppable, passionate soul winner? Your Heavenly Father has brought the "know how" to you through this wonderful book: "THE SHAKING AND THE GLORY". Prepare to soar!

**REV. YINKA OJO**
*(Grace Family Intl. Church, Lagos)*

A timely book for this end time army! If we must partake of the Glory to come then we must be shaken out of the deep slumber that has overwhelmed the body of Christ.

We must be thoroughly shaken and must shake ourselves from the dust of the ungodly, unscriptural and wordily influences that we have been entangled with and arise to righteousness and true Holiness.

This book is a must for everyone that want to be a part of the Glory to come. Thank you Rev Bolanta for yielding to the Holy Spirit in writing this book. He that have ears let him hear what the Spirit is saying

**Dr. MICHAEL OBIORA**
*Word Alive Ministry*
*Calabar. Nigeria*

Prophetic, profound, and potent, "The Shaking & the Glory" makes a compelling case for the church to raise an elite company of believers who will step out in spiritual authority and triumph over the forces of darkness that have been unleashed by an enemy who knows his time is short. Racy, direct, and full of gems of revelation, you can sense the urgency in the Spirit as you read this book.

Dr. Tunde Bolanta has done the larger Body of Christ a world of good with this treasure of a book, which brilliantly – and forcefully - sets forth the imperative for the church triumphant - a strong devotional life characterized by prayer, faithful study of the word, divine guidance, purity, faith and courage.

It is a must-read for every believer who truly desires to be victorious in every area of life. Unputdownable!

**Dr. JACKSON EKWUGUMBIBLE**
*Teacher & Publisher, Lifeway*

The title of Apostle Tunde Bolanta's Book, "The Shaking & The Glory" makes one's spirit water with expectation - and you won't be disappointed! He builds this literary masterpiece on a 3-fold combination of firstly, the living 'Rhema' prophecies he has received building up to the goings on in this present era; he then relates this to the times we are at the time of publishing this book - in the middle of a world-wide pandemic.

He then proceeds with a third essential building block of excellently articulating a biblical framework for 'shakings' and the intent of The FATHER in using them – for His ultimate purposes.

One cannot read this book without carrying a sense of the fearful (but also potentially glorious!) thing it is to 'fall into the hands of the living GOD'.

I whole heartedly recommend this as a manual for being prepared for this 'kairos' hour!

**ROBIN JEGEDE-BRIMSON**
*Inter Prophetic & Apostolic Alliance (IPAA)*
*Nigeria Academy of Prophetic & Apostolic Reform (NAPAR)*
*Author, "The Blaze of Transition"*

# Chapter One

# PROPHETIC PURPOSE
# OF SHAKING

The action of something or someone being shaken is often not a positive experience. Shaking could be the result of a trauma, or the disturbance of peace or the equilibrium in an environment.

When there is an earthquake, the earth trembles and it is a very unnerving experience. A few minutes before, the ground was stable, and now its trembling or convulsing right underneath your feet. In an aircraft, when turbulence is experienced, the plane could experience shaking, passengers are usually advised to put on a seat belt, to avoid being displaced or falling out of their seats.

According to Merriam Webster online dictionary, the word 'Shake' is defined as a blow or shock that upsets the equilibrium, disturbs the balance of something, to vibrate especially as the result of a blow or shock - and to tremble as a result of physical or emotional disruption.

Shaking has a negative connotation, but in scriptural terms, it is a special time when God uses crisis to catapult the believer to another level of grace. The Holy Spirit allows His servants to go through periods of shaking and the wilderness experience as a preparation for greater seasons ahead.

When God allows a shaking, He has beautiful plans to manifest Himself in a greater dimension in and through His people. Hebrews 12:26-28 reveals a shaking which would precede a great move of God.

**Hebrews 12:26-28**

*"Whose voice, then shook the earth: but now he hath promised, saying, Yet once more I shake not the earth only, but also heaven. And this word, Yet once more, signifieth the removing of those things that are shaken, as of things that are made, that those things which cannot be shaken may remain. Wherefore we receiving a kingdom which cannot be moved, let us have grace, whereby we may serve God acceptably with reverence and godly fear:"*

There is a great concern about the shaking of everything in our world at this time. Most people alive do not remember anything like it. It does not matter the time we live in, or the type of shaking that seems to affect believers and non- believers alike.

God's intention is to turn it around for his glory. His kingdom can never be shaken by anything in this world. It does not matter the storm or adversity God's purpose is to turn things around for his glory and his praise. Satan does not hold the key of God's end time agenda the blueprint is in the Father's hand and whatever the devil throws at the Church will be used as a stepping stone to move the Church into God's plan – God is always ahead of the devil.

The world was shut down as the Coronavirus, also known as COVID-19 took its toll on many around the world. Lives were lost, governmental functions were affected, stock markets were shocked, businesses shut down, sporting activities, economic activities, political events, Church meetings and public gatherings could not hold, normal life as we knew it, came to a screeching halt.

Everything that people built their lives around was shattered. It is reminiscent of the time that Egypt endured the ten plagues.

Their means of livelihood was affected, their gods could not help them. In the same vein, the gods of the world, the things the world idolized were paralyzed.

God did not create the evil virus, but he knew about it before it happened and allowed it as a wakeup call, to the Church and the world.

**Amos 3:7**
*"Surely the Lord GOD will do nothing, but he revealeth his secret unto his servants the prophets."*

God revealed the shaking to many prophets and his ministers prior to the manifestation of the pandemic. There are (were) several prophecies to this effect.

# HERE ARE EXCERPTS FROM
# PROPHECIES I RECEIVED
## Dec.31, 2019 & Jan. 5, 2020

*"Spiritual reawakening will start with shaking in the nations and in the church. Don't be worried about the shakings, the secrets revealed will lead to the removal of leaders in the church and the nation simultaneously.*

*The removal of candle sticks of churches and ministries would lead to realignment and repentance in the body of Christ ... The church will move more in authority and decrees as the "Ekklesia"- a governing body operating in spiritual authority. God ordained leaders will instruct the church to walk in dominion.*

*A decade where the church will rule and decree. The army of the Lord will take over. The Church will have the maturity to rule and reign, she will not be involved in human worship, idolatry and syncretism, which keeps the body of Christ in darkness. False leaders and shepherds will be removed, exposed and disgraced. God says, we should pray, because the time of judgments has come to this land. There is a rod of God going through the land right now.*

*And the Lord showed me from Ezekiel 37. He said there shall be a spiritual awakening. It will start with a shaking ... a noise in Nigeria, noise in the body of Christ. There will be noise, don't be worried about the shakings. Don't be worried about the secrets being revealed. Don't be worried about leaders being removed.*

*Don't be worried about the removal of candlesticks. It will lead to a re-awakening and a realignment and repentance will bring about revival in the land.*

*He said 2020 will be a year of realignment in every sphere in this nation, political realignment. People will say, but we have never seen this before, but things will begin to happen. There will be moving in every area, because I the Lord will shake it. He says; "once again, I the Lord will* shake the heavens, and I will shake the earth, so that the things that can be shaken, will be shaken. You know why I'm doing that, he said: You will know yourself that the finger of the Lord, has done this, because I will shake it and they will shake.

There are some people, you have thought are immovable. They are set like concrete, but when the shaking of heaven begins, I will shake all the shakable in spiritual, political and social life, because this is a kingdom nation and my hand is upon this nation, and my purpose shall be fulfilled.

It doesn't matter who gathers against your destiny, like a lion, I will roar, and I will conquer the wicked for you. I will release you into destiny. There shall be shaken in the church, there shall be shaking in the nation. No man or principality can stop it."

The word of the Lord has gone forth. That shaking will bring about realignment. I see God *connecting people of like minds together and they are beginning to work together. Judgment will start from the church. Be not afraid of the shaking that has been prophesied in the body of Christ, it will come because, I have given many opportunities to judge themselves, but they will rather jump into bed with the devil and eat of the table of idols; therefore I, the Lord, I'm going to call many of them home, so that the body of Christ can repent and there can be divine connections, bone finding its bone according to Ezekiel 37. I will see to it that my name is glorified.*

*The authentic move of the spirit will be seen in the church. Like the magicians of Egypt who performed false signs and wonders before Pharaoh, He said these present-day magicians and false prophets will be swallowed up in the shaking. There will be an authentic move of God in Nigeria and also in the body of Christ, globally.*

*I will remove the candlestick of people who have been disturbing my people in the church. I will shake the church one more time, and people will say it's the devil, but it is God working and revival will come, and there will be a realignment in my body, said the spirit of God.*

*The Lord says, this is a decade where the body will minister for the Lord as kings. They will make decrees and rule nations. I will begin to send you teachers and instructors and leaders in the body of Christ, locally and globally and who will instruct you.*

*Who will teach you how to stand on your authority in Christ. And one will chase a thousand, you will become so strong. One will put a thousand to flight and two will put ten thousand to flight. It's not going to be a decade of some few champions. You will not practice idolatry and syncretism in the church, but reign as kings in life.*

*I'm raising an elite army in the church in these last days an elite army that will bring down the works of the enemy. I'm raising the church and raising the bar and bringing the body of Christ to dominion, and the Gentiles will bow to the power, as the superior light will be seen in these last days, says the Spirit of the Lord. Maturity is coming to the church.*

*The church in Nigeria must be focused on her inheritance. Don't be carried away with the terror in the land. Did I not tell you, ask of me, and I will give you the heathen as your inheritance, and the uttermost parts of (the earth as your possession. Nigeria including Sambisa forest belongs to God.*

*I see angels descending like paratroopers, the Lord says, this nation is my nation. I'm sending a reinforcement of angels right now. Their job is to help you to advance. The stones of limitations have been rolled away. Come enjoy the things I have prepared for you.*

*The Lord says … I will strategically position my people because of the end time harvest, because I have proven them. It's the season for wealth, riches to sit in your house. I have proven your heart and I have seen that you want to push things into the kingdom.*

*There will be political lifts. Positions that you didn't seek for, will be offered. I will open doors to position you, because of the great harvest in front of you."*

PURPOSE OF SHAKING

**Heb 12:26**
*Whose voice, then shook the earth: but now he hath promised, saying, Yet once more I shake not the earth only, but also heaven.*

According to Strong's Concordance the word shake is the Greek *saleuō* which means to waver, that is, agitate, rock, topple or (by implication) destroy; figuratively, to disturb, incite - move, shake (together) ... stir up.

Why would God use a shaking which agitates, disturbs and stirs up? It signifies that God wants to change some things in the life of the believers. It is obvious to any sincere person that there have been shakings on a global scale, people have lost their lives, even believers have been affected, freedom has been limited, even the freedom to assemble but when God is involved, he works it out for good.

The first shaking referenced in Exodus 20 is that of Mount Sinai; when he came down, the mountain was up in smoke and the people were scared. They did not want to draw near to the mountain. Moses told them that God was doing this to put His fear in their hearts. Seasons of shaking are stormy seasons, they are times of tests and trials.

Jesus did not say that the believer, wouldn't go through those seasons, but he promised to bring the believer through and do a work inside the believer.

God wants to do a work in the believer at the time of shaking. He is calling for intimacy. The Lord Jesus was led into the wilderness by the Holy Spirit. One would wonder, the rationale behind sending Jesus straight from the baptism into the wilderness.

## SHAKING AND PERSONAL INTIMACY WITH THE FATHER

### Exodus 20:18 -21

*And all the people saw the thundering, and the lightning, and the noise of the trumpet, and the mountain smoking: and when the people saw it, they removed, and stood afar off. And they said unto Moses, "speak thou with us, and we will hear: but let not God speak with us, lest we die. And Moses said unto the people, Fear not: for God is come to prove you, and that his fear may be before your faces, that ye sin not. The God of Moses must become your God. And the people stood afar off, and Moses drew near unto the thick darkness where God was."*

Moses was eager to bring the children of Israel to mount Sinai, so they could have their own burning bush experience, but they were not ready. They would rather have Moses speak to them.

There is a Holy fear, an awesomeness of God that stays with you when you experience a genuine and authentic move of God for yourself. At the instance of shaking, you need to cultivate an intimate relationship with the father.

It is important that all believers are taught how to approach the father and experience deep intimacy. Those who do and have a revelation of the father's love are forever hooked to him.

Those who are only connected to great men of God, in time of crisis and isolation cannot reach God on their own. Moses also quaked, but he still went up the mountain, he was so desperate for intimacy with the father even if it would kill him.

## JESUS IN THE WILDERNESS

**Luke 4:1**
*And Jesus being full of the Holy Ghost returned from Jordan, and was led by the Spirit into the wilderness,*

**Luke 4:14**
*And Jesus returned in the power of the Spirit into Galilee: and there went out a fame of him through all the region round about*

**Hebrews 5:8**
*Though he were a Son, yet learned he obedience by the things which he suffered;*

**1Pet 5:10**
*But the God of all grace, who hath called us unto his eternal glory by Christ Jesus, after that ye have suffered a while, make you perfect, stablish, strengthen, settle you.*

Jesus was led by the Holy Spirit into the wilderness. Immediately, after the baptism and affirmation by the father, God sent him into the wilderness. A dry place, a place of demonic activity. The Lord Jesus did not sin, neither was he in disobedience.

This was all planned by heaven, when the devil felt that his physical body could be safely attacked. He tempted him. Jesus defeated the devil before he even started his ministry.

He returned in the power of the Spirit and his ministry continues to make an eternal impact. Jesus was in seclusion with wild animals all around him, Angels ministered to him as he faced Satan in a very hostile environment.

The Lord Jesus learnt obedience through the things he suffered, there are lessons that are learned in the tests and trials.

Smith Wigglesworth said, "*Great faith is the product of great fights. Great testimonies are the outcome of great tests. Great triumphs can only come out of great trials.*"

Jesus went through a violent storm with his disciples, he wanted them to learn to use the authority, he had given them. He wanted them to stop losing their peace in the storm. Jesus knew there was a storm, but he waited until the boat was getting full, he was waiting to see if one of them would step up and exercise dominion. They had spent considerable time hearing the word, now it was time for them to be graded.

Isaiah 41:10 says; "*In the furnace of affliction has he chosen me*" Other words for chosen is graded or branded me. How we fare in those times of shakings, those seasons of tests, show where we really are in our walk with God. The disciples doubted the love of God in the storm, they accused Jesus of not caring about them, they thought he was not mindful of the storm. Pressure brings the best and the worst out of people.

The lockdown is a time for believers to grow in intimacy with God, intercession, and exercising their authority over the storms of life. Jesus rebuked the storm and also rebuked them for not exercising their faith.

Jesus had faith in the disciples, he expected them to speak his words about going to the other side of the storm. He wanted them to speak to the storm.

They wondered what manner of man Jesus was that even the sea and the wind obeyed him. Jesus was telling them you could have done the same with the storm. They were expected to exercise their authority in the storm.

In the shaking, God wants to consume all that is not him in our lives until all that is seen is Him.

# A SHAKING IS A HOUSE CLEANING

## Hebrews 12:25-29 MSG

*"So don't turn a deaf ear to these gracious words. If those who ignored earthly warnings didn't get away with it, what will happen to us, if we turn our backs on heavenly warnings? His voice that time shook the earth to its foundations; this time – he's told us this quite plainly – he'll also rock the heavens" One last shaking, from top to bottom, stem to stern. The phrase "one last shaking" means a thorough housecleaning, getting rid of all the historical and religious junk so that the unshakable essentials stand clear and uncluttered. Do you see what we've got? An unshakable kingdom! And do you see how thankful we must be? Not only thankful, but brimming with worship, deeply reverent before God. For God is not an indifferent bystander. He's actively cleaning house, torching all that needs to burn, and he won't quit until it's all cleansed. God himself is a consuming fire!"*

In movies where professionals are invited to clean house, the amount of junk and clutter in the houses is usually staggering. Things are hidden between furniture, wardrobes are over flowing with useful and non-useful things that ought to have been discarded long ago.

There are things everywhere and you wonder how people move around the house, how those who live in there, make it to the bed. Those who live with the clutter seem to have adapted to it over time and they seem to be in their element.

According to Hebrews 12:29, when there is a shaking, God wants to remove historical and religious junk. The goal of the shaking is to make sure that the church, the 'Ekklesia' is fit for the glory that is ahead.

In order for the church to move in corporate glory, the church must no longer be tossed to and fro. The church must come into a season of experiential knowledge of God. The goal of ministry gifts, is to train the body of Christ to do the work of ministry. Like coaches, they prepare the team to win.

Unfortunately, many modern-day leaders need a paradigm shift in this regard - being more interested in a crowd, rather than in making disciples. Churches need to become discipleship centres where elite armies are raised.

I personally say to those close to me, "my goal is to make sure that you can do what I am doing so I can move on to other things". Leadership must be secure enough to transfer the deposits of the kingdom to believers who can keep the multiplication process going.

# Chapter Two

# REPENTANCE AND CONSECRATION

**Act 3:19**

*"Repent ye therefore, and be converted, that your sins may be blotted out, when the times of refreshing shall come from the presence of the Lord".*

**Joel 2:15-17**

*"Blow the trumpet in Zion, sanctify a fast, call a solemn assembly: Gather the people, sanctify the congregation, assemble the elders, gather the children, and those that suck the breasts: let the bridegroom go forth of his chamber, and the bride*

*out of her closet. Let the priests, the ministers of the LORD, weep between the porch and the altar, and let them say, spare thy people, O LORD, and give not thine heritage to reproach, that the heathen should rule over them: wherefore should they say among the people, where is their God?"*

The season of shaking is a season to sanctify a fast and seek the Lord. The heathen must not mock the church and wonder about the much talked about healing and miracle power of God. The demonstration of the healing and miracle power of God is not to make any minister a hero but rather to express the love of God to a suffering world.

It is rather disgraceful when some backslidden ministers stage manages miracles and this has now become public knowledge. At the time of a pandemic like this, you read of mockery in the media when the unsaved mock the miracle power of God. The miracle power of God is the same, in the midst of a crisis, be it a pandemic, family challenges, financial upheavals or whatever is creating the disquiet, that affects and threatens the peace in a believer's life.

God's power remains the same, it is another opportunity to put faith in His faithfulness and love. The genuine, authentic, ageless power of God is still available; nothing is too hard for the creator of the universe, the Father of mercies who is eagerly waiting, itching to do good. He specializes in impossibilities.

There are many false anointed servants of God in the world today. Some are well celebrated because of the wealth and the crowd they draw, but Jesus said he would say to some, I do not know you. Jesus also said by their fruit you shall know them.

**Mat 7:15 -23**
*"Beware of false prophets, which come to you in sheep's clothing, but inwardly they are ravening wolves. Ye shall know them by their fruits. Do*

*men gather grapes of thorns, or figs of thistles?
Even so every good tree bringeth forth good fruit;
but a corrupt tree bringeth forth evil fruit. A good
tree cannot bring forth evil fruit, neither can a
corrupt tree bring forth good fruit. Every tree
that bringeth not forth good fruit is hewn down,
and cast into the fire. Wherefore by their fruits ye
shall know them. Not everyone that saith unto
me, Lord, Lord, shall enter into the kingdom of
heaven; but he that doeth the will of my Father
which is in heaven.*

*Many will say to me in that day; Lord, Lord, have
we not prophesied in thy name? And in thy name
have cast out devils? And in thy name done
many wonderful works? And then will I profess
unto them, I never knew you: depart from me, ye
that work iniquity."*

Thorns don't produce grapes, a pineapple
plant cannot produce mango, an apple tree
does not produce oranges. When the
lifestyle of a minister produces falsehood,
adultery, manipulation, witchcraft and the

like Jesus said, that fruit is not representing his kingdom. Ministers can miss it and fall but when a minister perpetually lives the life of sin, he is not reflecting the kingdom of God.

Jesus continues the discussion by saying that not all those who say to him or reference him as Lord really belong to him, if their fruit is contrary to the character or nature of Jesus Christ. Many will say they did miracles in his name and prophesied in his name and he would reply them "I never knew you."

**Matthew 7:22-23 TPT**

*"On the day of judgment many will say to me, 'Lord, Lord, don't you remember us? Didn't we prophesy in your name? Didn't we cast out demons and do many miracles for the sake of your name?' But I will have to say to them, 'Go away from me, you lawless rebels! I've never been joined to you!"*

One thing is very clear from what Jesus said, he was not impressed with the success of the ministers in question because their lifestyles did not show the fruit of righteousness. In the words of Jesus, a thorn bush cannot produce grapes. They did not have the kingdom life reflected in them. They demonstrated miracles alright, but no life of Christ was seen. They were workers of iniquity, they had a lifestyle of sin.

It is difficult to fathom how a person can claim to be a minister of the Lord Jesus Christ and live like the devil. Let us consider a few possible conclusions. A minister that backslides and sears his conscience can live a life of iniquity and be no different from an unbeliever in daily conduct. Sin continued can create a seared conscience.

A backslidden minister's conscience is no longer a safe guide he can fall into unbelievable wickedness and become an impediment, a stumbling block to the body of Christ. Some ministers have come out to publicly repent after dabbling in the occult for church growth and success. When you hear these types of stories you find it hard to believe that a born-again child of God with a calling would condescend to use Satan's power to work for God.

I have come across a few cases where ministers have been desperate for so called breakthroughs and were willing to compromise. One of the ministers said to me that Jesus actually appeared to him at the witch doctor's place and he told him, "if you go through with the ritual you will no more be mine". He did not go through but there were other senior ministers who were patronizing the same evil altar.

**1Tim 4:1-2**
*"Now the Spirit speaketh expressly, that in the latter times some shall depart from the faith, giving heed to seducing spirits, and doctrines of*

*devils; Speaking lies in hypocrisy; having their conscience seared with a hot iron"*.

**1Tim 1:19-20**
*"Holding faith, and a good conscience; which some having put away concerning faith have made shipwreck: Of whom is Hymenaeus and Alexander; whom I have delivered unto Satan, that they may learn not to blaspheme."*

This is the reason why syncretism of traditional African religion and Christianity has become pronounced on the continent of Africa.

Traditional religion relies heavily on the use of fetish objects as a means of making spiritual connections with the spirit realm. In the Bible objects are symbolic.

In the New Testament James writes that the sick should be anointed with oil, but it is the prayer of faith that saves the sick. Jesus spat on the ground and made mud one time as recorded in scripture. He mainly spoke the word of God after they came to hear and be healed.

**James 5:14-15**

*"Is any sick among you? Let him call for the elders of the church; and let them pray over him, anointing him with oil in the name of the Lord: And the prayer of faith shall save the sick, and the Lord shall raise him up; and if he has committed sins, they shall be forgiven him."*

Many more churches have tied miracles to objects such as water, oil, soap, sand, honey, salt, hair comb, leaves, fruits, washing of feet, anointed chairs, minister's pictures, drinks, coconut and the like.

There are always different things like these on sale. The people's faith is not in the word of God, but in these things. A person going for an interview who forgets any of these talismanic objects has no confidence because his confidence was not in the word of God.

These unfortunate developments have made it difficult on the continent of Africa to differentiate between Bible believing churches and modern cult prayer houses.

Many use the same objects and display them as their so-called faith extenders. For some it is a way to raise money, while others are in covenant with the occult and use these fetish elements to contact evil spirits who are promoting their ministries.

There are those who are actually occult people from the start but realized that people who are religious would submit easier if they used a church building for their services. Jesus said when he returns, would he find faith on the earth? These people preach another gospel and another Jesus.

**2Cor 11:4**
*"For if he that cometh preacheth another Jesus, whom we have not preached, or if ye receive another spirit, which ye have not received, or*

*another gospel, which ye have not accepted, ye might well bear with him."*

These preach another Jesus, the Jesus they preach is dictatorial, oppressive and manipulative. Paul humbled himself and served, but others came with big egos and the Corinthian church cowered before them.

Those preaching another Jesus have another spirit, they are only after their stomachs and they boast about material abundance. They do not have any ongoing relationship with Christ. They are backslidden or have never known the Lord.

Their gospel is a gospel of self and merchandise. It is not about souls, but how much they make. They only move based on a financial arrangement. Comfort comes before service, many use ministry opportunities to further the lifestyle of immorality.

## Mark 13:6

*"For many shall come in my name, saying, I am Christ; and shall deceive many."*

Jesus warned that many would come on that day and say I am Christ. The word 'am' is the same root word for the word 'ego'. Today, the advertisement and exaggeration of fake ministers are unbelievable. They fake results, fake miracles, their egos are all people gather to see. Some are entertainers in cahoots with the occult.

The word Christ is the word Christos according to Strong's Concordance G5548; meaning, anointed; that is, the Messiah, an epithet of Jesus - Christ.

False and backslidden ministers major on the anointing and not the fruit. They emphasize their power but their lifestyles do not reflect Christ. Sadly, there are those who do not mind receiving power from the devil. Evil spirits can facilitate healings, there is a counterfeit for every gift of the Holy Spirit. This explains why there are no fruits but continuous talk of the anointing, miracles and prophecies.

It is important that the body of Christ walks in discernment and take note of ministries that are not walking in the fruit of the Holy Spirit so that believers will not make shipwreck of their faith.

I had a revelation of my brother who passed to glory during a Sunday morning worship in church about the time of the second anniversary of his death. He was excited and looked to the earth with little interest. He said, ' I am happy I made it, many I expected here are not here'

The notion that once people are born again, they are forever saved and can live like the devil is not scriptural. Paul the Apostle said, he puts his body under so that after preaching to others he himself will not be a castaway.

## CONSECRATION

### Daniel 3:20 - 30

*"And he commanded the most mighty men that were in his army to bind Shadrach, Meshach, and Abednego, and to cast them into the burning fiery furnace. Then these men were bound in their coats, their hosen, and their hats, and their other garments, and were cast into the midst of the burning fiery furnace. Therefore, because the king's commandment was urgent, and the furnace exceeding hot, the flame of the fire slew those men that took up Shadrach, Meshach, and Abednego. And these three men, Shadrach, Meshach, and Abednego, fell down bound into the midst of the burning fiery furnace. Then Nebuchadnezzar the king was astonied, and rose up in haste, and spake, and said unto his counsellors; Did not we cast three men bound into the midst of the fire? They answered and said unto the king, True, O king. He answered and*

*said, Lo, I see four men loose, walking in the midst of the fire, and they have no hurt; and the form of the fourth is like the Son of God. Then Nebuchadnezzar came near to the mouth of the burning fiery furnace, and spake, and said, Shadrach, Meshach, and Abednego, ye servants of the most high God, come forth, and come hither. Then Shadrach, Meshach, and Abednego, came forth of the midst of the fire. And the princes, governors, and captains, and the king's counsellors, being gathered together, saw these men, upon whose bodies the fire had no power, nor was a hair of their head singed, neither were their coats changed, nor the smell of fire had passed on them. Then Nebuchadnezzar spake, and said, blessed be the God of Shadrach, Meshach, and Abednego, who hath sent his angel, and delivered his servants that trusted in him, and have changed the king's word, and yielded their bodies, that they might not serve nor worship any god, except their own God. Therefore, I make a decree; That every people, nation, and language, which speak anything amiss against the God of Shadrach, Meshach, and*

*Abednego, shall be cut in pieces, and their houses
shall be made a dunghill: because there is no other
God that can deliver after this sort. Then the king
promoted Shadrach, Meshach, and Abednego, in
the province of Babylon.*

Shadrach, Meshach, and Abednego were of
unparalleled consecration. They took up
their cross, they refused to bow and worship
the golden image. It looked like their very
end.

The church of Jesus Christ needs to be
hardened to persecution; saints must be
ready to go into the fiery furnace if required.
The three Hebrews knew God could deliver
them, but if he did not deliver them they
would not bow.

There is a message that says 'once you come
to Jesus you would float through life with no
suffering and no challenges. This is wrong.
Truly you cannot suffer what Christ suffered
because he suffered for the whole world as a

substitute but you must take your own share of suffering by taking up your cross every day and following Jesus. The church tries not to be offensive to the world, in fact, seeker sensitive churches do not want the Holy Spirit in demonstration so as not to offend the world.

Churches try to pattern their music and setting to reflect the world but the Holy Spirit will not manifest when the goal is to be an alternative entertainment centre. We need to be reminded that the early church paid with their lives to bring the gospel to other generations. Everyone listed in Hebrew 11, is there because of their faith, their sacrifices and the risk they took in order to do the will of God.

REVERENTIAL FEAR AND GLORY

**Hebrews 12:28-29**
*"Wherefore we receiving a kingdom which cannot be moved, let us have grace, whereby we*

*may serve God acceptably with reverence and godly* fear: For our God is a consuming fire."

Divine encounters create reverence for God, Moses was forever changed by the burning bush experience. God wanted the children of Israel to experience him personally.

Anyone who has a genuine encounter with God is always desirous of more of God. An encounter with the Lord leaves a yearning for the authentic.

The presence of God will burn off the chaff out of believers leaving what is genuine behind. The presence is consuming of sin but purifies those who are sincerely longing for God.

Ananias and Sapphira died in the glory because they lied when they ought to have repented.

# SHAKING IS THE BELIEVERS BOOT CAMP

**Act 19:9-10.**

*"But when divers were hardened, and believed not, but spake evil of that way before the multitude, he departed from them, and separated the disciples, disputing daily in the school of one Tyrannus. And this continued by the space of two years; so that all they which dwelt in Asia heard the word of the Lord Jesus, both Jews and Greeks."*

**Acts 19:8-9 AMPC**

*"And he went into the synagogue and for three months spoke boldly, persuading and arguing and pleading about the kingdom of God. But when some became more and more stubborn (hardened and unbelieving), discrediting and reviling and speaking evil of the Way [of the Lord] before the congregation, he separated himself from them, taking the disciples with him, and went on holding daily discussions in the*

*lecture room of Tyrannus from about ten o'clock till three."*

Paul seemed to hit a brick wall with opposition and hindrances to the furtherance of the gospel so he decided to major on making the believers disciples. This strategy was so successful that the whole area heard the gospel.

I remembered being opposed seriously for teaching believers how to heal the sick because some ministers at the time felt this was taking away ministers' jobs and giving it to the laity. The church that will cut across cultural and religious barriers like those in the school of Tyrannus are genuine disciples who practice authentic Christianity.

Paul the Apostle was simply reproducing himself in these disciples. His style was always to leave deposits in the life of disciples that would help them stand in the face of persecutions from within and without. The church of the first century was birthed in persecution but full of power and grace.

Paul and the apostles had to be deliberate and authentic in their approach to ministry. Their goal was not to entertain, they needed to build a spiritual army that would not fear adversity, an army that was ready for confrontation and rejoiced in persecution.

An army that knew how to pray to release angels into warfare. The school of Tyrannus was an intensive boot camp. Paul called himself a master strategist. He knew that the hardness of the terrain and the opposition to the gospel he was facing needed nothing less than well trained disciples who would make other disciples.

**2 Timothy 2:1-6 AMPC**
*"SO YOU, my son, be strong (strengthened inwardly) in the grace (spiritual blessing) that is [to be found only] in Christ Jesus. And the*

*[instructions] which you have heard from me along with many witnesses, transmit and entrust [as a deposit] to reliable and faithful men who will be competent and qualified to teach others also. Take [with me] your share of the hardships and suffering [which you are called to endure] as a good (first class) soldier of Christ Jesus. No soldier when in service gets entangled in the enterprises of [civilian] life; his aim is to satisfy and please the one who enlisted him. And if anyone enters competitive games, he is not crowned unless he competes lawfully (fairly, according to the rules laid down). [It is] the hardworking farmer [who labours to produce] who must be the first partaker of the fruits."*

Paul expected those under his tutelage to be prepared to suffer hardship. There are trainings that produce endurance; when athletes train to produce endurance, they are hard on themselves; certain that on the day of competition they will be successful. I have followed the success stories of some African athletes from developing countries on the world stage. There is a common trend in their stories.

Many grew up in rural African communities where they had to trek far to get water and then trek several miles to school on very difficult terrains. Some had to run most of the way to arrive in their schools on time.

Those with this background have endured hardship and difficulty before coming on the world stage. Running on muddy, rocky slopes and hills prepared them for the canvas experience in a world class Stadium. The hard training makes it easy for them to succeed in the real contest.

God allows seasons of shakings to be times of separation for the Church. A time of soul searching, a time to remove the clutter. A time to draw close to him and prepare for the next level.

## PURSUIT OF HOLINESS: TAKING UP YOUR CROSS

In the season of shaking when God brings the believer into a time of seclusion and renewal of strength, he consumes all the chaff and the works of the flesh in the believer's life. The closer we come to God the more his fire begins to burn things out of our lives.

He is a consuming fire, His fire comes to remove every chaff and worthless things; the awesomeness of his presence brings about godly fear and creates a hunger to become more like him.

**Luke 9:23 - 27**
*"And he said to them all, If any man will come after me, let him deny himself, and take up his cross daily, and follow me. For whosoever will save his life shall lose it: but whosoever will lose his life for my sake, the same shall save it. For what is a man advantaged, if he gain the whole*

*world, and lose himself, or be cast away? For whosoever shall be ashamed of me and of my words, of him shall the Son of man be ashamed, when he shall come in his own glory, and in his Father's, and of the holy angels. But I tell you of a truth, there be some standing here, which shall not taste of death, till they see the kingdom of God."*

**1Cor 6:20**

*For ye are bought with a price: therefore, glorify God in your body, and in your spirit, which are God's.*

**Gal 2:20**

*"I am crucified with Christ: nevertheless I live; yet not I, but Christ liveth in me: and the life which I now live in the flesh I live by the faith of the Son of God, who loved me, and gave himself for me."*

**1Pe 4:1-2**

*"Forasmuch then as Christ hath suffered for us in the flesh, arm yourselves likewise with the*

*same mind: for he that hath suffered in the flesh hath ceased from sin; That he no longer should live the rest of his time in the flesh to the lusts of men, but to the will of God."*

Believers are reminded that we do not own ourselves, we actually signed our rights away when we received Jesus as Lord. On the cross we died with him, he took our place, our sin nature, all the attendant curses and he gave us his own life.

Supposing a man decides to give his functioning heart to a friend who needs a heart transplant on the condition that the receiving friend would live out the life and dreams of the donor. The beneficiary is alive but has to live the life of the donor.

Jesus took our place, gave us new life on the condition that we would live for him. He also in the new life gave us the power to live above sin and all the works of the enemy.

Taking up our cross daily means living to glorify God. Our old man died, the new man is Christ in us. The flesh may want to go the old way, but out of love for Jesus our flesh must be reminded that the life we live now is not our own. Daily taking up the cross means, willingness to suffer in the flesh.

It means the flesh will be uncomfortable, the flesh will protest, but the old man was nailed to the cross with Jesus. There is a new man on the inside which is Christ the hope of glory.

## SHAKINGS REVEAL WHAT CANNOT BE SHAKEN

**Removes Idols**

**Psalm 74:20**
*"Have respect unto the covenant: for the dark places of the earth are full of the habitations of cruelty."*

**Hebrews 12:26, 27**

*"Whose voice, then shook the earth: but now he hath promised, saying, Yet once more I shake not the earth only, but also heaven. And this word, Yet once more, signifieth the removing of those things that are shaken, as of things that are made, that those things which cannot be shaken may remain."*

In the season of tests and shakings, the focus of the church should be on what cannot be shaken. The covenant in the blood of Jesus, the power of the Holy Spirit, the word of God, the love of God and our redemption is eternally settled.

Spiritual leaders may fail or fall in a shaking, but remember that Jesus is still on the throne, his kingdom cannot be shaken, that kingdom is within you because he lives within the believer by the power of the Holy Spirit and the believer shall not be shaken. The time of shaking is a time to reaffirm our faith in the unshakable God, his word and our unshakable covenant through the blood of Christ our substitute. The time of shaking is a time to return to authenticity because when there is a shaking, all false things fall off.

**Hebrews 12:27-29**

*"And this word, Yet once more, signifieth the removing of those things that are shaken, as of things that are made, that those things which cannot be shaken may remain. Wherefore we receiving a kingdom which cannot be moved, let us have grace, whereby we may serve God acceptably with reverence and godly fear: For our God is a consuming fire."*

REVERENTIAL FEAR OF GOD

The early church was in revival, souls were being added, mighty miracles were happening in the midst of persecution but suddenly, there was a shaking. The higher the intensity of glory the higher the shaking. Ananias and Sapphira sold a portion of land

and lied that they had brought the entire sum and both fell dead in the service.

### Act 5:1-11

*"But a certain man named Ananias, with Sapphira his wife, sold a possession, and kept back part of the price, his wife also being privy to it, and brought a certain part, and laid it at the apostles' feet. But Peter said, Ananias, why hath Satan filled thine heart to lie to the Holy Ghost, and to keep back part of the price of the land? Whiles it remained, was it not thine own? And after it was sold, was it not in thine own power? Why hast thou conceived this thing in thine heart? Thou hast not lied unto men, but unto God.*

*And Ananias hearing these words fell down, and gave up the ghost: and great fear came on all them that heard these things. And the young men arose, wound him up, and carried him out, and buried him. And it was about the space of three hours after, when his wife, not knowing what was done, came in. And Peter answered unto her, Tell me whether ye sold the land for so much? And she said, Yea, for so much. Then Peter said unto her, How is it that ye have agreed together to tempt the Spirit of the Lord? Behold, the feet of them which have buried thy husband are at the door, and shall carry thee out. Then fell she down straightway at his feet, and yielded up the ghost: and the young men came in, and found her dead, and, carrying her forth, buried her by her husband. And great fear came upon all the church, and upon as many as heard these things."*

The more the glory, the higher the consecration must be. These two died because the presence of God was very strong. The fear of God definitely increased among them - those who were not really committed to the cause of Christ would not bother becoming part of this elite army.

The standard of holiness and demonstration of the spirit was very high. The Holy Spirit was interested in adding quality to the church. We need to pray for the restoration of the fear of God, to the degree that the ungodly would be weary of playing church.

Many years ago in my undergraduate days, I went to a university to minister and had given a word of knowledge and the wrong person stood up. I asked him to seat sown, but he insisted. Before all of us, just a few meters towards me, the power of God lifted him off the ground. It brought a reverence for God to the meeting.

KING DAVID IN AWE OF GOD

The ark had been in the house of Abinadab. Uzzah and Ahio were his sons who were familiar with the ark as it had been in their home. Their home had prospered, but they did not follow the protocol for carrying the ark.

Priests were supposed to carry the ark, it was not to be on a cart. Therefore, when they came to the threshing floor of Nachon, the oxen shook the ark and Uzzah tried to steady the cart. He died on the spot. David was afraid of the Lord.

As the Lord restores more of his glory after the season of shaking, the church must be aware of the protocols in the glory. We cannot do what we want, when we want it, without paying attention to the word of God and the Holy Spirit. A threshing floor is a place where the harvest is prepared, an uneven place

**2 Sam 6:1-9**

*"Again, David gathered together all the chosen men of Israel, thirty thousand. And David arose, and went with all the people that were with him from Baale of Judah, to bring up from thence the ark of God, whose name is called by the name of the LORD of hosts that dwelleth between the cherubims. And they set the ark of God upon a new cart, and brought it out of the house of Abinadab that was in Gibeah: and Uzzah and Ahio, the sons of Abinadab, drave the new cart.*

*And they brought it out of the house of Abinadab which was at Gibeah, accompanying the ark of God: and Ahio went before the ark. And David and all the house of Israel played before the LORD on all manner of instruments made of fir wood, even on harps, and on psalteries, and on timbrels, and on cornets, and on cymbals. And when they came to Nachon's threshing floor, Uzzah put forth his hand to the ark of God, and took hold of it; for the oxen shook it. And the anger of the LORD was kindled against Uzzah; and God smote him there for his error; and there he died by the ark of God. And David was displeased, because the LORD had made a breach upon Uzzah: and he called the name of the place Perezuzzah to this day. And David was afraid of the LORD, that day, and said, How shall the ark of the LORD come to me?"*

## HARDENED TO PERSECUTION, PASSIONATE ABOUT SOULS

The Lord Jesus was unequivocal when he told his disciples that persecution was a part and parcel of the deal for those who would follow him. The history of the early church shows that they were severely persecuted and in an attempt to escape persecution they spread their faith abroad.

Jesus promised to bless and reward those who follow him in this world with persecution. They counted it an honour to be found worthy to suffer persecution for the Lord. The apostles were flogged, imprisoned and killed for their faith. The mentality the early church possessed was that of an elite army who were ready for combat.

They rejoiced to 'suffer shame' for the gospel. The apostle Paul wrote that those who would live godly must be prepared to suffer persecution. Paul said he did not count his life important, there was nothing too much for him to give up.

In Asia, Paul was not sure of his life, so aggressive was the attack that it looked like he would not make it. His training was thorough, he accepted that persecution would go with the proclamation of the gospel. He trusted God for deliverance and he was delivered and the enemy could not touch him until the work was done.

# Chapter Three

# TRAINING OF AN ELITE ARMY

It is only a fake soldier that does not expect war. The training for those combatant men can be gruelling. Why is that? Because when they are in the real theatre of war, the enemies will not be firing plastic bullets at them.

The church must recognize that as we enter into the last of the last days, our enemy is going to be more brazen and fierce as Satan is setting up the stage for the emergence of the anti-Christ. The time of training is mightily inconvenient for the soldiers, they are secluded and must follow a tough and thorough regimen just like athletes who desire success have to punish their bodies. Paul said he punished his body so he would not be a castaway.

I believe the time of shaking globally by reason of the present corona pandemic shall be accompanied by the great harvest of souls. It is a time of preparation for a great harvest but the crowd must become an army. The church must be reminded that Satan will use any situation to bring restrictions to the church and slow down the great commission.

The Lord in a vision on the third of November 2019 told me he had come to open the sheep gate. It is time for the greatest harvest of souls but the troops must be prepared. The church was birthed in persecution and exploded during persecution. We need to raise believers who know how to endure persecution, reap the harvest of souls, walk in the protection of the Lord and who are also ready to lay down their lives if necessary.

I know of places on the front lines where hundreds of churches were destroyed by terrorists with Christians burnt alive and three to four years down the line there are more churches and believers in the same places. What sort of believers are in these places?

In these last days, we must raise an army of believers who do not stick with Jesus out of convenience and whose motivation is not Church entertainment.

An elite army of believers who have an ongoing intimate and passionate relationship with the Lord Jesus, people who are filled with the Holy Spirit. A church that is not bound down to fetish elements and human worship but is solely committed to the word of God. Faith that costs you nothing means nothing.

The army that would reap the harvest in the midst of persecution must be well grounded. This army must know the weapons of her warfare and be skilful in using the weapons. Everyone listed in Hebrews 11 is there because he was delivered or he overcame something and made sacrifices.

### 1Peter 5:10 AMPC

*"And after you have suffered a little while, the God of all grace [Who imparts all blessing and favour], Who has called you to His [own] eternal glory in Christ Jesus, will Himself complete and make you what you ought to be, establish and ground you securely, and strengthen, and settle you."*

A settled believer must be ready to take his share of suffering not disease, not poverty, but he must be willing to pay whatever price he needs to pay when his flesh stands in the way of fulfilling God's purpose. A believer who is not ready to deny the flesh is not ready to take up his cross.

A look at the scriptures that follow is a reminder that to be settled is to arm ourselves to suffer in the flesh rather than fail to please God. Pleasing God is a choice we make. We are born again and given the power to live above sin and walk in dominion.

Persecution should be seen as part and parcel of the bargain. Believers should not fear resistance. I know of places where bombs went off on a previous Sunday and the church had more people attending service after the bomb blast.

There are towns on the Frontlines where hundreds of churches were destroyed and four years down the line there are more churches in the same town. The believers were determined that persecution would not stop them.

### John 5:18-20

*"If the world hate you, ye know that it hated me before it hated you. If ye were of the world, the world would love his own: but because ye are not of the world, but I have chosen you out of the world, therefore the world hateth you. Remember the word that I said unto you, The servant is not greater than his lord. If they have persecuted me, they will also persecute you; if they have kept my saying, they will keep yours also."*

### Act 5:40-42

*"And to him they agreed: and when they had called the apostles, and beaten them, they commanded that they should not speak in the name of Jesus, and let them go. And they departed from the presence of the council, rejoicing that they were counted worthy to suffer shame for his name. And daily in the temple, and in every house, they ceased not to teach and preach Jesus Christ."*

## 2Cor 1:8-11

*"For we would not, brethren, have you ignorant of our trouble which came to us in Asia, that we were pressed out of measure, above strength, insomuch that we despaired even of life: But we had the sentence of death in ourselves, that we should not trust in ourselves, but in God which raiseth the dead: Who delivered us from so great a death, and doth deliver: in whom we trust that he will yet deliver us; Ye also helping together by prayer for us, that for the gift bestowed upon us by the means of many persons thanks may be given by many on our behalf."*

## Luke 21:10-19

*"Then said he unto them, Nation shall rise against nation, and kingdom against kingdom. And great earthquakes shall be in diverse places, and famines, and pestilences; and fearful sights and great signs shall there be from heaven. But before all these, they shall lay their hands on you, and persecute you, delivering you up to the synagogues, and into prisons, being brought before kings and rulers for my name's sake. And*

*it shall turn to you for a testimony. Settle it therefore in your hearts, not to meditate before what ye shall answer: For I will give you a mouth and wisdom, which all your adversaries shall not be able to gainsay nor resist. And ye shall be betrayed both by parents, and brethren, and kinsfolks, and friends; and some of you shall they cause to be put to death. And ye shall be hated of all men for my name's sake. But there shall not an hair of your head perish. In your patience possess ye your souls."*

## 2 Timothy 3:10-13

*"But thou hast fully known my doctrine, manner of life, purpose, faith, longsuffering, charity, patience, Persecutions, afflictions, which came unto me at Antioch, at Iconium, at Lystra; what persecutions I endured: but out of them all the Lord delivered me. Yea, and all that will live godly in Christ Jesus shall suffer persecution. But evil men and seducers shall wax worse and worse, deceiving, and being deceived."*

**Act 4:23-31**

*"And being let go, they went to their own company, and reported all that the chief priests and elders had said unto them. And when they heard that, they lifted up their voice to God with one accord, and said, Lord, thou art God, which hast made heaven, and earth, and the sea, and all that in them is: Who by the mouth of thy servant David hast said, Why did the heathen rage, and the people imagine vain things? The kings of the earth stood up, and the rulers were gathered together against the Lord, and against his Christ. For of a truth against thy holy child Jesus, whom thou hast anointed, both Herod, and Pontius Pilate, with the Gentiles, and the people of Israel, were gathered together, For to do whatsoever thy hand and thy counsel determined before to be done. And now, Lord, behold their threatenings: and grant unto thy servants, that with all boldness they may speak thy word, By stretching forth thine hand to heal; and that signs and wonders may be done by the name of thy holy child Jesus. And when they had prayed, the place was shaken where they were assembled together;*

and they were all filled with the Holy Ghost, and
they spake the word of God with boldness."

### Act 15:25-26

"It seemed good unto us, being assembled with
one accord, to send chosen men unto you with
our beloved Barnabas and Paul, Men that have
hazarded their lives for the name of our Lord
Jesus Christ."

### Act 20:24

"But none of these things move me, neither count
I my life dear unto myself, so that I might finish
my course with joy, and the ministry, which I
have received of the Lord Jesus, to testify the
gospel of the grace of God."

### 1 Peter 5:10 AMPC

"And after you have suffered a little while, the
God of all grace [Who imparts all blessing and
favour], Who has called you to His [own] eternal
glory in Christ Jesus, will Himself complete and
make you what you ought to be, establish and

*ground you securely, and strengthen, and settle you."*

**2Cor 4:7-9**

*"But we have this treasure in earthen vessels, that the excellency of the power may be of God, and not of us. We are troubled on every side, yet not distressed; we are perplexed, but not in despair; Persecuted, but not forsaken; cast down, but not destroyed."*

**2Cor 11:24-28**

*"Of the Jews five times received I forty stripes save one. Thrice was I beaten with rods, once was I stoned, thrice I suffered shipwreck, a night and a day I have been in the deep; In journeyings often, in perils of waters, in perils of robbers, in perils by mine own countrymen, in perils by the heathen, in perils in the city, in perils in the wilderness, in perils in the sea, in perils among false brethren; In weariness and painfulness, in watchings often, in hunger and thirst, in fastings often, in cold and nakedness. Beside those things*

*that are without, that which cometh upon me daily, the care of all the churches."*

**Rev 12:11**

*"And they overcame him by the blood of the Lamb, and by the word of their testimony; and they loved not their lives unto the death."*

## GROOMING OF LEADERS AND THE WILDERNESS

**Moses In the Wilderness**: *Character Moulding and Vision*

**Act 7:29-30**

*"Then fled Moses at this saying, and was a stranger in the land of Madian, where he begat two sons. And when forty years were expired, there appeared to him in the wilderness of mount Sina an angel of the Lord in a flame of fire in a bush."*

Moses ran away as a fugitive, then he settled in Midian after marrying Jethro's daughter.

He spent forty years on the backside of the desert herding his father in law's flock.

Moses was very passionate about his convictions, he identified with his Jewish background and was not ashamed of it. Although he was raised as Pharaoh's son, he was quick to defend an Israelite against an Egyptian.

Once the murder of the Egyptian was known, he had to flee. In the desert God was dealing with him to remove self-righteous indignation. So, thorough was the dealing of God that when he was offered the assignment of a deliverer, he was unwilling to go back to Egypt.

The wilderness is a place character is moulded. It is a place of solitude, sober reflection and renewal of strength. It was the divine encounter of the burning bush that renewed Moses strength to move into the call upon his life. Moses before the wilderness and Moses after the wilderness presents a journey of personal transformation. Moses was the meekest man after the dealings of God in the wilderness.

## PAUL IN THE WILDERNESS: DEEPER REVELATION

**Gal 1:17,18**

*"Neither went I up to Jerusalem to them which were apostles before me; but I went into Arabia, and returned again unto Damascus. Then after three years I went up to Jerusalem to see Peter, and abode with him fifteen days."*

The time Paul spent in Arabia has been dubbed the silent years. This was a time of seclusion when he waited on God for his ministry. Some of the revelations in the epistles were received at this time of separation. What is the use of a wilderness experience?

Paul has a glorious conversion when he was blinded by the light on his way to Damascus to waste the church. He was one hundred percent for the devil and his passion for the Lord after salvation was total.

In Damascus, after his eyes were opened, he immediately started preaching and they planned to kill him. God needed to deepen Paul's relationship, discernment and character. As he graduated from the wilderness university, his ministry touched lives and the impact is still ongoing in the world today.

**Act 9:19-22**

*"And when he had received meat, he was strengthened. Then was Saul certain days with the disciples which were at Damascus. And straightway he preached Christ in the synagogues, that he is the Son of God. But all that heard him were amazed, and said; Is not this he that destroyed them which called on this name in Jerusalem, and came hither for that intent, that*

*he might bring them bound unto the chief priests? But Saul increased the more in strength, and confounded the Jews which dwelt at Damascus, proving that this is very Christ."*

## ELIJAH IN THE WILDERNESS

### 1Kings 19:1-4

*"And Ahab told Jezebel all that Elijah had done, and withal how he had slain all the prophets with the sword. Then Jezebel sent a messenger unto Elijah, saying, So let the gods do to me, and more also, if I make not thy life as the life of one of them by to morrow about this time. And when he saw that, he arose, and went for his life, and came to Beersheba, which belongeth to Judah, and left his servant there. But he himself went a day's journey into the wilderness, and came and sat down under a juniper tree: and he requested for himself that he might die; and said, It is enough; now, O LORD, take away my life; for I am not better than my fathers."*

## A PLACE OF REFRESHING

Elijah took off running after Jezebel threatened to end his life, he went a day's journey further into the wilderness. He was ready to die. God strengthened him with angel food and he arrived at the mountain of God. An angel was sent to refresh Elijah.

Sometimes a minister or believer can just be weary from spiritual battle fatigue. God understood that. After the refreshing Elijah went to Horeb and was strengthened for forty days and night. God reminded him he had seven thousand that had not bowed their knees to Baal. Elijah received the blue print about his assignment and the passing of the baton to the next generation.

## QUIET AND SOBER REFLECTION

The wilderness is a place of quiet, sober reflection and a place to hear the voice of God. Elijah felt he was a Lone Ranger, but

God tried to lift his sight, he told Elijah, he had seven thousand that had not bowed to Baal. Elijah was obviously not aware of the remnant. He had no active contact with them.

When a believer or minister experiences battle fatigue, he becomes weary from contending with so much opposition; spiritual, mental, emotional and physical, there is a tendency to be so stressed, such that the believer is unable to see the bigger picture.

Elijah wanted to preserve his life, he felt lonely and wanted his misery to end. God directed him on how to hand over to the next generation, but he needed to go to Horeb to hear God.

Believers and ministers alike need a place away from the hustle and bustle of life, a place where they are quiet in their minds, an environment where they are not easily distracted. In a season when movements are limited or in more recent times when people are quarantined because of a pandemic, this is a great opportunity to refresh, refocus and re-fire. In such a season, the Holy Spirit can help believers to look at challenges with fresh eyes.

KNOWING THE HOLY SPIRIT:

Elijah came to Horeb expecting the spectacular. Whenever we are alone with God, separated from the noise around, God is always eager to show us more of himself. Clearly, Elijah expected spectacular demonstrations like what happened on mount Carmel when fire came down but God wanted to shift his paradigm.

The voice of God was not in the wind, the earthquake, nor the fire, but he was in the still small voice. Elijah was experiencing the glory of God in another dimension. He had seen fire dramatically fall from heaven and consume the sacrifice but in his crisis moment God was in a still small voice. The wilderness is a place where the walk with God is deepened.

The Holy Spirit has been sent as our helper, what an opportunity when there is a shaking to draw on Him who created the universe, what a privilege to drink from the wells of the Spirit who raised Jesus from the dead. Jesus said of the Holy Spirit:

**John 15:26**
*"But when the Comforter is come, whom I will send unto you from the Father, even the Spirit of truth, which proceedeth from the Father, he shall testify of me."*

Comforter: Greek: paraklētos: An intercessor, consoler: - advocate, comforter."

**John 15:26 AMPC**
*"But when the Comforter (Counselor, Helper, Advocate, Intercessor, Strengthener, Standby)*

*comes, Whom I will send to you from the Father,
the Spirit of Truth Who comes (proceeds) from
the Father, He [Himself] will testify regarding
Me."*

**Rom 8:26-28**

*"Likewise, the Spirit also helpeth our infirmities:
for we know not what we should pray for as we
ought: but the Spirit itself maketh intercession
for us with groanings which cannot be uttered.
And he that searcheth the hearts knoweth what is
the mind of the Spirit, because he maketh
intercession for the saints according to the will of
God. And we know that all things work together
for good to them that love God, to them who are
the called according to his purpose."*

**Jude 1:20**

*"But ye, beloved, building up yourselves on your
most holy faith, praying in the Holy Ghost."*

The Holy Spirit is the most patient and
gentle person I know, he loves passionately
and is always longing to minister to the

believer and through the believer. One of the ways to stay connected and energized by the Holy Spirit is by praying in other tongues. The Holy Spirit energizes the human spirit to pray.

Believers have the privilege of tapping into the knowledge of God through the Holy Spirit. The Holy Spirit, the source and custodian of all knowledge, prays through the believer, this means the believer is always praying the will of God.

There is no hindrance to the throne of grace. The Holy Spirit allows you to tap into the reservoir of God's knowledge. You pray beyond your weaknesses.

Praying in the Holy Spirit will help you turn adversity to triumph. Through intercession by the help of the Holy Spirit, you pray for the unknown. You uproot wicked plans of the enemy against you.

PRAYING IN THE HOLY SPIRIT IS REFRESHING.

**Isa 28:11-12**
*"For with stammering lips and another tongue will he speak to this people. To whom he said, this is the rest wherewith ye may cause the weary to rest; and this is the refreshing: yet they would not hear."*

Isaiah speaks prophetically about a stammering tongue and a refreshing, I believe it refers to praying in tongues. There is a refreshing, a rest, a catching of breath when believers pray in the Holy Spirit. There is a rest on the inside that brings a renewal of the whole person.

Praying in the Spirit can also be likened to sharpening a knife or a weapon against a stone the way they did in the old days. The stone the weapon rubs against will give the weapon the sharpness to be effective. The psalmist prayed about going to a higher rock at the time of crisis. The cutting edge needed in times of stress is available when the believer prays in the Holy Spirit.

ISRAEL IN THE WILDERNESS

**Deut 8:2**
*And thou shalt remember all the way which the LORD thy God led thee these forty years in the wilderness, to humble thee, and to prove thee, to know what was in thine heart, whether thou wouldest keep his commandments, or not."*

The wilderness is a place of testing, God took Israel through the wilderness to prove them or test them ahead of what was ahead. The place of testing precedes the place of promotion.

Often times, it is in the season of pressure that what is hidden is revealed. The shaking is to remove or make known the things hidden so that when promotion comes the believer is ready for the next level. Abraham was tested when he was told to sacrifice his son whom he loved. He passed the test because he obeyed at once and was willing and ready to kill Isaac as a burnt offering until God showed up and stopped him.

He told him he passed the test and something bigger was ahead, a promotion, he would be a blessing to the whole world but the test preceded the promotion. His obedience meant God could take the covenant relationship for the salvation of mankind to another level.

God stopped him from killing Isaac but reaffirmed to him that all the nations of the world would be blessed through him as God would send his own son through the lineage of Isaac to die as a substitute for mankind.

**Genesis 22:10-18**
*"And Abraham stretched forth his hand, and took the knife to slay his son. And the angel of the LORD called unto him out of heaven, and said,*

*Abraham, Abraham: and he said, Here am I. And he said, Lay not thine hand upon the lad, neither do thou any thing unto him: for now I know that thou fearest God, seeing thou hast not withheld thy son, thine only son from me. And Abraham lifted up his eyes, and looked, and behold behind him a ram caught in a thicket by his horns: and Abraham went and took the ram, and offered him up for a burnt offering in the stead of his son. And Abraham called the name of that place Jehovah Jireh: as it is said to this day, In the mount of the LORD it shall be seen. And the angel of the LORD called unto Abraham out of heaven the second time, And said, By myself have I sworn, saith the LORD, for because thou hast done this thing, and hast not withheld thy son, thine only son: That in blessing I will bless thee, and in multiplying I will multiply thy seed as the stars of the heaven, and as the sand which is upon the sea shore; and thy seed shall possess the gate of his enemies; And in thy seed shall all the nations of the earth be blessed; because thou hast obeyed my voice."*

# DIGGING YOUR OWN WELLS

## Gen 26:13 -21

*"And the man waxed great, and went forward, and grew until he became very great: For he had possession of flocks, and possession of herds, and great store of servants: and the Philistines envied him. For all the wells which his father's servants had digged in the days of Abraham his father, the Philistines had stopped them, and filled them with earth. And Abimelech said unto Isaac, Go from us; for thou art much mightier than we. And Isaac departed thence, and pitched his tent in the valley of Gerar, and dwelt there. And Isaac digged again the wells of water, which they had digged in the days of Abraham his father; for the Philistines had stopped them after the death of Abraham: and he called their names after the names by which his father had called them. And Isaac's servants digged in the valley, and found there a well of springing water. And the herdmen of Gerar did strive with Isaac's herdmen, saying, The water is ours: and he called the name of the well Esek; because they strove with him. And*

*they digged another well, and strove for that also: and he called the name of it Sitnah."*

Isaac was supernaturally led to stay in Gerar and not go down to Egypt. He was favoured and he reaped one hundred-fold in a season of famine and drought. The Philistine envied him and sent him away.

He began digging again wells that were dug by his father which had been filled with sand and they contended with him. Believers may face envy and rejection, they may be ostracized by their family and community. This challenge would force believers to depend on God and their identity in Christ for survival.

Abraham had dug these wells in times past. Abraham dug deep in challenging times to find water to sustain him. A true reawakening is finding the old wells and finding the secrets for the strength of those who went ahead of us. Isaac was now the leader of the family, he needed to find his strength in God just the same way his father did. When the believer is facing a test and is alone, God must become his God.

The testimonies he had heard must become his own testimony. It is a time of personal spiritual adventure, hard work in line with your spiritual heritage. Elijah had to pour water on the sacrifice, something from the old was needed as foundation to enter into the new, water is precious in the wilderness and in times of famine.

Naming the wells by the name they were called shows that Isaac had a revelation and recognized ancient landmarks. It is easy to read other people's sermon but the most powerful word is one you have experienced yourself.

Following those who through faith and patience inherited the promises is a scriptural principle, but walking in the revelation for yourself is what stabilizes you. Isaac suffered rejection but he had to learn by digging the same wells his father dug. He found his strength in God. He left Ezek which means strife in Hebrew and Sitnah meaning hostility or hatred.

This shows that he realized that his inheritance would be given by the grace of God not by strife, contention, hatred and hostility. The servant of God must not strive, the wilderness or time of testing helps us to realize what is in our heart in this area.

His father Abraham had the same attitude when there was strife between the herdsmen of his nephew and his own herdsmen, he allowed Lot to choose first, he avoided strife at all costs after which God appeared to him and reaffirmed the covenant.

Persistence in digging shows that he believed the blessing was upon him and he, not the ground, determine the outcome. The season of seclusion and testing are times for re-evaluation. A lot of natural people may have fought for those wells and maybe they could have been killed. Isaac demonstrates that the blessing was on him.

The location, land, estate needed him more than he needed them. The blessing, the oil, the grace was upon him because of the covenant, so if he had to dig a hundred wells he would keep finding water.

He kept moving until he dug another well and this time they did not strife with him about it and he called it Rehoboth. This was his place of rest. Persistence produce rest. His testimony was that the Lord had made room for him. When the Lord makes room, no man can stop your wells.

Those who do not believe that persecution is part of the deal might quit at the slightest threat of opposition. We have built churches in places where they gather dangerous weapons and the team is told to leave before morning or else prepare to give their lives if the building is started but with much prayer churches are standing in those places. If no one is persecuting or opposing you, maybe you are not a danger to the enemy.

Isaac could have used this as an excuse to go elsewhere or head for Egypt which was his original idea. When you have not received a new directive from the commander in chief just stay at your post; he knows where he sent you. Staying around Gerar was difficult, the kings and the nobles had thrown Isaac out, the wells of his father were filled with sand, hostility and rejection was everywhere he turned.

The visitation of the Lord after the period of shaking was a divine pointer that he was on track and a marker for the future. The shaking will remove what needs to be removed, it is much like using a sieve, it removes the worthless from the precious. A period of testing is a good time to be intimate with God, lay our motives on his altar, spend time communing in the word and by the Holy Spirit and be prepared to be released into the next level in the power of the Holy Spirit.

Enduring the period of shaking will cause your profiting to appear before all men and reconcile your enemies to you. Abimelech the king and his leaders came to Isaac after all the tests to make a covenant with him.

God honours those who endure the tests, tough times, rejection, bitterness and hatred with a godly attitude; he makes their enemies to be at peace with them.

**Gen 26:22 , 24-33**
*"And he removed from thence, and digged another well; and for that they strove not: and he called the name of it Rehoboth; and he said, For now the LORD hath made room for us, and we shall be fruitful in the land."*

**Gen 26:24-33**

*"And the LORD appeared unto him the same
night, and said, I am the God of Abraham thy
father: fear not, for I am with thee, and will bless
thee, and multiply thy seed for my servant
Abraham's sake. And he builded an altar there,
and called upon the name of the LORD, and
pitched his tent there: and there Isaac's servants
digged a well. Then Abimelech went to him from
Gerar, and Ahuzzath one of his friends, and
Phichol the chief captain of his army. And Isaac
said unto them, Wherefore come ye to me, seeing
ye hate me, and have sent me away from you?
And they said, We saw certainly that the LORD
was with thee: and we said, Let there be now an
oath betwixt us, even betwixt us and thee, and let
us make a covenant with thee; That thou wilt do
us no hurt, as we have not touched thee, and as
we have done unto thee nothing but good, and
have sent thee away in peace: thou art now the
blessed of the LORD. And he made them a feast,
and they did eat and drink. And they rose up
betimes in the morning, and sware one to*

*another: and Isaac sent them away, and they departed from him in peace. And it came to pass the same day, that Isaac's servants came, and told him concerning the well, which they had digged, and said unto him, We have found water. And he called it Shebah: therefore, the name of the city is Beersheba unto this day."*

# Chapter Four

# YOU ARE GOD'S BATTLE AXE

**Jeremiah 51:20 ASV**

*"Thou art my battle-axe and weapons of war: and with thee will I break in pieces the nations; and with thee will I destroy kingdoms."*

Isa 41:14

*"Fear not, thou worm Jacob, and ye men of Israel; I will help thee, saith the LORD, and thy redeemer, the Holy One of Israel."*

**Isa 41:15**

*"Behold, I will make thee a new sharp threshing instrument having teeth: thou shalt thresh the mountains, and beat them small, and shalt make the hills as chaff."*

**Eph 6:10 -18**

*"Finally, my brethren, be strong in the Lord, and in the power of his might. Put on the whole armour of God, that ye may be able to stand against the wiles of the devil. For we wrestle not against flesh and blood, but against principalities, against powers, against the rulers of the darkness of this world, against spiritual wickedness in high places. Wherefore take unto you the whole armour of God, that ye may be able to withstand in the evil day, and having done all, to stand. Stand therefore, having your loins girt about with truth, and having on the breastplate of righteousness; And your feet shod with the preparation of the gospel of peace; Above all, taking the shield of faith, wherewith ye shall be able to quench all the fiery darts of the wicked. And take the helmet of salvation, and the sword*

*of the Spirit, which is the word of God: Praying always with all prayer and supplication in the Spirit, and watching thereunto with all perseverance and supplication for all saints."*

The end time army must be skilled because the enemy knows his time is short hence his aggressiveness. This is the responsibility of the ministry gifts, to train believers and bring them to maturity.

The heart of believers must be established in the word, they must all be taught about how they can go to the throne of grace on their own. When Moses brought the children of Israel out of Egypt, he wanted them to have their own burning bush experience similar to his own encounter.

He told them God brought them to the mountain to 'prove' them so his fear will be in their hearts but they were too afraid to go near God. The church in some parts of the body of Christ is still in the same dilemma today.

Some would rather pray to the God of their man or woman of God rather than see God as their own.

**Hebrews 5:13**
*"For every one that useth milk is unskillful in the word of righteousness: for he is a babe."*

**Hebrews 5:14**
*"But strong meat belongeth to them that are of full age, even those who by reason of use have their senses exercised to discern both good and evil."*

**Exodus 20:19 -21**
*"And they said unto Moses, Speak thou with us, and we will hear: but let not God speak with us, lest we die. And Moses said unto the people, Fear not: for God is come to prove you, and that his fear may be before your faces, that ye sin not. And*

*the people stood afar off, and Moses drew near unto the thick darkness where God was."*

It is not a New Testament practice to pray in the name of the God of any man or woman of God. In the Old Testament, the anointing rested on the prophets, the priests and the king. The people needed to go to them or to the tabernacle to make contact with God through the priesthood.

In the New Testament however, all born again believers are welcome to the throne because of the blood of Jesus that has redeemed the church and made a way. Jesus as the high priest of the new covenant is the mediator between God and man.

The church can only approach the throne in the name of Jesus and through his blood. The blood had to be sprinkled heavenward and was accepted. Every note that was written against us was cancelled because it was the perfect blood on the highest altar by the highest being. No human being has any credit outside the blood of the lamb to approach the throne of God.

To have people pray in the name of any man of God, no matter how successful, is idolatry. I had an experience somewhere overseas where people started to sell my picture as a point of contact for miracles. I was grieved and immediately stopped them. People's faith must not be misplaced.

Ministers are called to help believers to do the same miracles they see in the ministry gifts. Ministers are called to train believers to engage in prayers and get their prayers answered. They should be taught how to cast out devils, practice intercession and walk in dominion. The believers must understand their ministries as priests and kings.

In a season of crisis or shaking, believers who have been trained to develop a personal relationship with God will use the period as a time of refreshing and renewal of strength. They will engage in worship, intercession, study and meditation of the word and will plant precious seeds of mercy into the lives of others.

As they minister in times of challenges to others such believers will never be stranded or bewildered. The church is the people not the four walls of a building, it is a living, thriving body of believers, who are alive, every minute of the day and night.

A force for God that cannot be contained, an army of Eagles that fear no storm and no foe. Those who were men of God and fetish element dependent are usually left stranded because they did not develop an ongoing relationship with the Lord.

In a time of crisis, it is your relationship with God that sustains you, not your relationship with the God of the man of God.

Those whose Christianity has been reduced to elements such as oil, water, soap, honey, salt, pictures and the like; have no root in the time of crisis.

Believers must connect with the living Christ, connect with his word, learn to lean on the Holy Spirit and make the word first place. Such believers are unstoppable and a danger of the devil.

**Eph 6:10**
*"Finally, my brethren, be strong in the Lord, and in the power of his might."*

**Eph 6:11**
*"Put on the whole armor of God, that ye may be able to stand against the wiles of the devil."*

The believer is equipped to be a weapon in the hand of God when he puts on God's armour. The believer is God's battle axe as long as the believer abides in God. There is no victory outside of God. The believer is not told to be strong in himself, but in the Lord. The believer's life is hid in Christ, he is the vine, we are the branches. The branch of a tree is absolutely useless outside of the tree. Jesus told the disciples that outside of him, they could do nothing, a branch that is disconnected from the trunk would gradually rot away. The secret to power is to abide in him.

## THE WHOLE ARMOUR OF GOD

An armour or weapon gives you an advantage and you operate from a superior position. If someone confronts you with an AK 47, you immediately recognize that he is at an advantage except you have a higher calibre weapon.

The age of an assailant does not matter if he is seated in a military armoured tank. You are careful because of his superior advantage. When the believer puts on God's armour he is in a superior position to the enemy. This armour has been proven by God himself and known to work all the time. Believers must learn to take advantage of the armour of God to win the battles of life.

Paul the Apostle was inspired to use the Roman soldier's outfit. They were well dressed, every armour in place. A rag tag army cannot win the battle, such an army is a disgrace to the nation it represents.

The whole armour is a reminder of complete preparation, dressed to kill and defend. In real warfare, Satan is not firing blank bullets at the army, if the Lord must prepare for real warfare, we must be ready for some shakings.

There are seasons of shakings where God prepares the army for what is ahead. There is a season of seclusion where the eagle must pluck her feathers and her beak, she is forced on a fast and is restored by growing new feathers and beak and elongates her life and effectiveness.

## Eph 6:11-12

*"Put on the whole armour of God, that ye may be able to stand against the wiles of the devil. For we wrestle not against flesh and blood, but against principalities, against powers, against the rulers of the darkness of this world, against spiritual wickedness in high places."*

God's Spiritual armours have been proven to defeat invincible enemies. The battle is against invincible forces; there are real physical challenges present which have their roots in the spirit. The forces of fear, depression, rejection, anger, infirmity and the like are all controlled by evil spirits.

There are seasons when such attack may be more apparent and increased. Such times the believer needs to delve deeper in the word, learn to use his authority and seek more mentoring where necessary.

I remember a young man visiting me at a place I served many years ago. One day he rushed down to me in total hysteria he described a terrible experience. A human head appearing in the wall spoke to him and asked him what he was doing in this location.

The young believer just wanted to leave and get away as far as possible but I was living at that location and at the same time ministering the word. I personally felt that he ought to have stayed, spent time in prayer and confronted that demonic spirit if it ever showed up again.

Whatever we are afraid of will Lord it over us. If the devil is under our feet, according to Jesus then we must experience and walk in dominion.

We moved to our present campus some years ago and ran into demonic attacks. While we were purchasing the property, the chief told me that the stream flowing through the property emptied into a river that took a life yearly so we needed to be strong.

When we took possession of the property people would come and stand under trees because they believed their destinies were tied by evil spirits to the trees. It is believed that witches and demonic spirits used the trees in the Church garden as a place of meeting.

People who lived on the campus had a lot of vivid nightmares. We also experienced flooding which damaged a lot of things. One day while in prayer I was in the spirit and suddenly saw the goddess of the river on the banks of the river, she confronted me directly.

I rebuked her in Jesus name and she dissolved and was broken into pieces by a lightning from above. After this encounter all the demonic, physical and spiritual attacks ceased.

### Eph 6:13

*"Wherefore take unto you the whole armour of God, that ye may be able to withstand in the evil day, and having done all, to stand."*

### Ephe 6:13 AMPC

*"Therefore put on God's complete armour, that you may be able to resist and stand your ground on the evil day [of danger], and, having done all [the crisis demands], to stand [firmly in your place]."*

The believer requires the whole armour to stand firmly in the battles of life. Some crisis tends to dislodge people from their places in the sense that people may come out with scars because their shield of faith was not in place, or they begin to question their identity because the breastplate of righteousness was not well seated. A total body armour means that whatever is thrown at the believer, he is battle ready and battle hardened to come out in victory and move to the next level.

## THE BELT OF TRUTH

**Eph 6:14**
*"Stand therefore, having your loins girt about with truth, and having on the breastplate of righteousness."*

**John 17:17**
*"Sanctify them through thy truth: thy word is truth."*

*Example:* Believing a lie means you fight the wrong battles. The aim of prayer is defeated. The belt of truth entails your covenant in Christ and it holds the other weapons in place. It is your ground for victory in every crisis.

If you have used a trouser or pants that uses a rope as support at its waistline or belt you immediately understand that if the rope weakens, the trouser slackens or falls down. That is a big issue. It is equally true that when the belt of truth is not there your trousers will fall and you will be embarrassed.

The Roman belt armour also had other weapons hung to it. When the belt of truth is not there you lose weapons hanging on the belt.

Jesus calls the word of God the truth. It sanctifies or sets you apart. The belt prevents disgrace as long as it holds and the nakedness of the believer is covered. As long as the belt is in place the believer's mind is guarded from the lies of the enemy.

**1Pet 1:13**
*"Wherefore gird up the loins of your mind, be sober, and hope to the end for the grace that is to be brought unto you at the revelation of Jesus Christ."*

## TRUTH VERSUS FACTS

The battleground is the mind where the enemy launches missiles after missiles of proven facts against the believer's mind. The facts of life are diametrically opposed to the truth of God's word.

The truth sets free because the word of God is forever established. The word is a law that is forever established in heaven. It is a light that darkness cannot overcome. It is the law of life, an established principle that cannot be overcome.

There are natural laws that are established and there is nothing that can be done against them, all man needs to do is cooperate with them. The law of gravity says what goes up must come down but the law of aerodynamics is able to lift a heavy airplane up by combining the law of lift and thrust thus overcoming the law of gravity.

Similarly, the law of faith is a superior law to the law of fear. It cancels it by releasing faith in the word of God and the finished work of Calvary.

**Psalm 119:89**
*"For ever, O LORD, thy word is settled in heaven."*

**John 17:17**
*"Sanctify them through thy truth: thy word is truth."*

**Psalm 119:165**
*"Great peace have they which love thy law: and nothing shall offend them."*

**Prov. 6:23**
*"For the commandment is a lamp; and the law is light; and reproofs of instruction are the way of life."*

**Rom 8:2**

*"For the law of the Spirit of life in Christ Jesus hath made me free from the law of sin and death."*

**2Cor 13:8**

*"For we can do nothing against the truth, but for the truth."*

**1Sam 17:31-36**

*"And when the words were heard which David spake, they rehearsed them before Saul: and he sent for him. And David said to Saul, Let no man's heart fail because of him; thy servant will go and fight with this Philistine. And Saul said to David, Thou art not able to go against this Philistine to fight with him: for thou art but a youth, and he a man of war from his youth. And David said unto Saul, Thy servant kept his father's sheep, and there came a lion, and a bear, and took a lamb out of the flock: And I went out after him, and smote him, and delivered it out of his mouth: and when he arose against me, I caught him by his beard, and smote him, and slew him. Thy servant slew both the lion and the bear:*

*and this uncircumcised Philistine shall be as one
of them, seeing he hath defiled the armies of the
living God."*

David a teenager faced Goliath who was a
man of war with many years of experience.
Goliath was a giant, the armies of Israel were
so scared stiff they ran away. The natural
equation was against David. Goliath
employed the satanic weapon of fear. He
disdained David

**1Sam 17:42**

*"And when the Philistine looked about, and saw
David, he disdained him: for he was but a youth,
and ruddy, and of a fair countenance."*

According to Strong's concordance Disdain:
bâzâh: ': A primitive root; to: - despise,
disdain, contemn, think to scorn. The
Hebrew word means to scorn, despise;
Goliath from the natural felt a kid like David
was no match for him. He told David he

would annihilate him. David went with the truth of the covenant to face Goliath.

There are things that you are facing right now that in the natural you feel outnumbered and powerless against but with the truth of God's word in your heart and constantly meditating, thinking of the word your mind will be renewed to the victory made possible for you through the finished work of Christ on the cross and the word that cannot fail.

The word cannot fail because God upholds all things by the power of his word. The word cannot fail because God and his word are one. The word cannot fail because Jesus is the word manifested in the flesh.

The word cannot fail because it has pleased God to highly exalt the word above his name.

## BREASTPLATE OF RIGHTEOUSNESS: YOUR IDENTITY

### Eph 6:14

*"Stand therefore, having your loins girt about with truth, and having on the breastplate of righteousness."*

### 1Sa 17:31 -37

*"And when the words were heard which David spake, they rehearsed them before Saul: and he sent for him. And David said to Saul, Let no man's heart fail because of him; thy servant will go and fight with this Philistine. And Saul said to David, Thou art not able to go against this Philistine to fight with him: for thou art but a youth, and he a man of war from his youth. And David said unto Saul, Thy servant kept his father's sheep, and there came a lion, and a bear, and took a lamb out of the flock: And I went out after him, and smote him, and delivered it out of his mouth: and when he arose against me, I caught him by his beard, and smote him, and slew him. Thy servant slew both the lion and the bear:*

*and this uncircumcised Philistine shall be as one
of them, seeing he hath defied the armies of the
living God. David said moreover, The LORD
that delivered me out of the paw of the lion, and
out of the paw of the bear, he will deliver me out
of the hand of this Philistine. And Saul said unto
David, Go, and the LORD is with thee."*

David did not argue with Goliath that he
was just a boy, he did not argue about his
lack of military experience, he did not try to
convince his brothers that he was qualified.
He reminded all that he had a covenant that
Goliath did not have.

The covenant is what determines your
identity. It is who you are in the spiritual.
Abraham his forefather believed God and it
was counted to him for righteousness.

He had a right standing with God because of
the agreement between Abraham through
the blood of animals and circumcision.
Abraham entered a new agreement with

- 149 -

God through the covenant that gave him a right standing with God. He promised to bless those that bless him and curse those that curse him. Through the blood covenant he became a friend of God and his offspring who bore the circumcision.

Men were qualified to draw supernatural help and favour from God in any crisis of life. This was David's premise for the battle. Although all the soldiers of Israel were circumcised they had no revelation of the victory through the covenant.

The breastplate in a soldier's armour protects all the vital organs of the body. They protect the heart and lung and vital organs in the region of the thorax. Any harm to those organs would be terminal. The soldier's life depends on it.

## THE IDENTITY OF THE BELIEVER IS IN THE COVENANT.

**Phil 3:3**
*"For we are the circumcision, which worship God in the spirit, and rejoice in Christ Jesus, and have no confidence in the flesh."*

**1Pet 2:9**
*"But ye are a chosen generation, a royal priesthood, a holy nation, a peculiar people; that ye should show forth the praises of him who hath called you out of darkness into his marvellous light."*

**1Pet 2:10**
*"Which in time past were not a people, but are now the people of God: which had not obtained mercy, but now have obtained mercy."*

**Col 2:11-12**
*"In whom also ye are circumcised with the circumcision made without hands, in putting off the body of the sins of the flesh by the*

*circumcision of Christ: Buried with him in baptism, wherein also ye are risen with him through the faith of the operation of God, who hath raised him from the dead."*

The believer is circumcised in the heart when he receives Jesus Christ as his Lord and Saviour. There is a mark in the spirit that he is a child of God. Believers are the people of God because we were raised together with Jesus as his body - we share the same DNA.

As believers identify with Jesus, the realization dawns that we were with him on the cross because he went there as our representative. All our sins, the attendant curses, the wrath and the judgement he received, we also received as his body, when he went to hell we also went with him and when he arose, we rose with him.

Our identity that gives us the right to stand before God is the blood covenant between

Jesus and God in our behalf. Jesus agreed to be our substitute. In other words, he agreed to take our place and has made us the family of God.

David had the revelation of Abraham and God making a covenant in his behalf. He knew he was circumcised and God was with him. Four days prior, twice daily the challenge of Goliath had gone unanswered until David showed up.

He did not plan to look for Goliath. It was all in the line of family duties. His father had sent him with supplies to his older brothers in the battle field.

Revelation is not determined by natural age but by your relationship with God. He said, God had helped him earlier to slay both the lion and the bear and was sure that the same revelation of his identity would be sufficient to cut off Goliath's head.

The breastplate of righteousness is critical because on your own you are no match for the devil. The devil will bring up your past failures and lapses. The word of God you have proven will work again and again. The word is the supreme authority.

David could not use Saul's armour because he had not proven them. In order to have an exciting walk with the Lord, confront your fears with the word of God. David did not allow the devil to intimidate him with negative words because words paint pictures.

The more you listen to the word the better the inner picture of your victory you will see. Don't be silent, speak your redemption, declare your identity and God will make it good.

**1Sam 17:38-51**
*"And Saul armed David with his armour, and he put a helmet of brass upon his head; also he armed*

*him with a coat of mail. And David girded his sword upon his armour, and he assayed to go; for he had not proved it. And David said unto Saul, I cannot go with these; for I have not proved them. And David put them off him. And he took his staff in his hand, and chose him five smooth stones out of the brook, and put them in a shepherd's bag which he had, even in a scrip; and his sling was in his hand: and he drew near to the Philistine. And the Philistine came on and drew near unto David; and the man that bare the shield went before him. And when the Philistine looked about, and saw David, he disdained him: for he was but a youth, and ruddy, and of a fair countenance. And the Philistine said unto David, Am I a dog, that thou comest to me with staves? And the Philistine cursed David by his gods. And the Philistine said to David, Come to me, and I will give thy flesh unto the fowls of the air, and to the beasts of the field. Then said David to the Philistine, Thou comest to me with a sword, and with a spear, and with a shield: but I come to thee in the name of the LORD of hosts, the God of the armies of Israel, whom thou hast* defied. *This day will the LORD deliver thee into mine hand; and I will smite thee, and take thine head from thee; and I will give the carcases of the host of the Philistines this day unto the fowls of the air, and to the wild beasts of the earth; that all the earth may know that there is a God in Israel. And all this assembly shall know that the LORD saveth not with sword and spear: for the battle is the LORD'S, and he will give you into our hands. And it came to pass, when the Philistine arose, and came and drew nigh to meet David, that David hasted, and ran toward the army to meet the Philistine. And David put his hand in his bag, and took thence a stone, and slang it, and smote the Philistine in his forehead, that the stone sunk into his forehead; and he fell upon his face to the earth. So, David prevailed over the Philistine with a sling and with a stone, and smote the Philistine, and slew him; but there was no sword in the hand of David. Therefore, David ran, and stood upon the Philistine, and took his sword, and drew it out of the sheath thereof, and slew him, and cut off his head therewith. And when the Philistines saw their champion was dead, they did field."*

 Paul had to use his Roman identity when he was being examined by scourging. He said to the centurion that it was unlawful to scourge a Roman citizen who was not condemned.

They stopped the scourging and were afraid. In the same manner when the believer recognizes his identity in Christ, he can stop the onslaught of hell. The devil knows that he has no right to scourge you a second time because Jesus already took the curse on our behalf.

The breastplate of righteousness is having a working knowledge of this reality. You declare that what Jesus paid for is yours because he conquered Satan for you and transferred the credit for his accomplishments for you to use.

If a friend decides to credit your account with a large amount of money, as soon as you receive an alert that the money is credited, it is no longer a promise, it is yours. All the promises are fulfilled in Christ because he paid the full price at Calvary. You can act like it is true, say so and act so.

**Act 22:24 -29**

*"The chief captain commanded him to be brought into the castle, and bade that he should be examined by scourging; that he might know wherefore they cried so against him. And as they bound him with thongs, Paul said unto the centurion that stood by, is it lawful for you to scourge a man that is a Roman, and uncondemn?"*

When the centurion heard that, he went and told the chief captain, saying, take heed what thou doest: for this man is a Roman. Then the chief captain came, and said unto him, Tell me, art thou a Roman? He said, Yea. And the chief captain answered, with a great sum obtained I this freedom. And Paul said, But I was free born.

Then straightway they departed from him which should have examined him: and the chief captain also was afraid, after he knew that he was a Roman, and because he had bound him.

The power of God manifested when he raised the believer up together with Jesus exceeds anything he had ever demonstrated.

**Eph 1:19**
*"And what is the exceeding greatness of his power to us-ward who believe, according to the working of his mighty power The Greek word for Exceeding: according to Strong's concordance means to 'throw beyond the usual mark, to surpass, to excel."*

God lifted the body of Christ, in a show of strength and power never before seen. It was his love in demonstration to have his family together. Whatever happens to the head happens to the body. You are a member of the body of Christ. As he is now, so are we in this world. An uncircumcised Philistine can not defeat Christ so they cannot defeat you. God has got your back because of the covenant. Remind yourself and the devil of who you are and whose you are. Paul told the people on his boat, although he was a prisoner in the ensuing crisis, he demonstrated to all that he was an ambassador; a man of covenant who is attended to by angels. You are not alone in the battle. Your blood covenant guarantees that God will fight on your side.

## FEET SHOD: BOOTS ON THE GROUND

**Eph 6:15**
*"And your feet shod with the preparation of the gospel of peace."*

The word Shod in the Greek means: to bind under one's feet, that is, put on shoes or sandals - bind on, be shod.

It means you need to have your shoes on, ready to be a witness. After Israel ate the Passover in haste, they were dressed for departure, ready to leave the bondage for freedom. I believe this weapon is an offensive weapon of soul winning.

The believer is to live ready. He needs to be dressed. The more we are witnesses for Christ, the stronger our testimony and the more of the move of God the believer will experience on a personal basis. One reason many believers have not seen the miraculous personally is that they are not ready, they are not hunting for souls.

They are not willing to declare what God has done in their lives they are hesitant to say to the unsaved that Jesus is not in the grave and he answers prayers and heals today just like he did in Bible days. When I received the Holy Spirit baptism I had no one to instruct me. I simply read that the Holy Spirit baptism will enable us to be witnesses.

I went everywhere looking forward to what the Holy Spirit will do as I testified about Jesus. This childlike faith paid great dividends. After sharing the gospel, I would ask if I could pray for any need because Jesus is still alive, I saw miracles after miracles.

**Isa 52:7**

*"How beautiful upon the mountains are the feet of him that bringeth good tidings, that publisheth peace; that bringeth good tidings of good, that publisheth salvation; that saith unto Zion, Thy God reigneth!"*

The early church exploded because persecution forced them out of their comfort zone. Everywhere they went they were ready to proclaim the gospel. They were the gospel on wheels. All believers must see their places of assignment as platforms for the good news. Jesus said the church was to go into the world and preach the gospel. Our worlds are different, some believers could be in the academia, manufacturing, social work, education, politics, home making and so on.

As the feet of Christ, wherever we go, the Lord has boots on the ground. He has an army there. When there are boots on the ground, the home country is out on notice, extra support and logistics are arranged. Many believers wish to see the miraculous - the way forward is to be the boots of Jesus on the ground, preach the gospel in season and out of season.

Every time foreign armies set foot in another country, their home countries are committed because they represent their home states. Once the armies put boots on the ground, the home country is on red alert to see that nothing goes wrong. They are prepared to deploy resources and whatever it takes to support them. One reason I believe some do not see deeper manifestations of the Holy Spirit is because their boots are not on the ground.

They work in different places with their jobs, but they are simply earning a living, they do not see themselves as ambassadors. They are not hunting for opportunities to be witnesses for Jesus, they work for their pay. It is important not to spend work time preaching but be true ambassadors who are witnesses in prayer silently looking for openings to be witnesses.

It could be during break times or when riding together, just beaming the love of God and being genuinely interested in people will enable God to show up. God will manifest when our purposes line up with him, he might give a vision or a word of knowledge about what a colleague is going through. When Jesus asked the woman of

Samaria for water she related to him in the natural until he had a word of knowledge about her present and her past, suddenly there was an opening. Do you have boots on the ground for Jesus?

# Chapter Five

# THE SHIELD OF FAITH

**Eph 6:16**
*"Above all, taking the shield of faith, wherewith ye shall be able to quench all the fiery darts of the wicked."*

The Greek word for shield denotes a large door shaped meaning weapon. This shield is large enough to cover the soldier. It is the first obvious target of the enemy when it is in place. The shield of faith is a defensive weapon that stops fiery attacks designed to steal your faith. It is lifted to cover everything.

The shield of faith is like the feathers of a duck, it keeps you from getting wet. In warfare, sometimes shields were soaked overnight in water so that when the fiery darts are thrown their fires are extinguished upon contact with the shield.

The shield of faith is essentially the word of God that has been digested and you are ready to use as a weapon in a season of crisis. Every test is designed to cause a crisis of faith. Life will ask questions which must be responded to in faith.

**Luke 22:31-34**

*"And the Lord said, Simon, Simon, behold, Satan hath desired to have you, that he may sift you as wheat: But I have prayed for thee, that thy faith fail not: and when thou art converted, strengthen thy brethren. And he said unto him, Lord, I am ready to go with thee, both into prison, and to death. And he said, I tell thee, Peter, the cock shall not crow this day, before that thou shalt thrice deny that thou knowest me."*

## THE SIEVING PROCESS

A sieve separates the authentic from the worthless. Peter did not humble himself when Jesus prophesied about his betrayal and he failed. Pressure reveals what is good and bad in us. Peter repented.

The true value of what is believed is revealed in the sieving process. Symptoms, bad report and fear targets your shield of faith and deny your redemption. The acronym for the word fear is, 'false evidence appearing real.' Fears are facts that challenge the truth of the word.

Fiery darts are darts that carry fire and they are very dangerous, these are thoughts that the enemy fires into the mind of the believer based on facts of life and scary circumstances but the word can be a defence in such as season.

**Hebrews 2:14**

*"Forasmuch then as the children are partakers of flesh and blood, he also himself likewise took part of the same; that through death he might destroy him that had the power of death, that is, the devil; And deliver them who through fear of death were all their lifetime subject to bondage."*

A pastor shared the testimony of a woman who through fear became depressed and suicidal. She turned on her radio and listened to me preach the word. She got hold of the messages, listened daily and all her fears disappeared.

Jesus took on human nature, went to the cross, became a curse and defeated Satan for us. There is nothing Satan is throwing as a dart of fear that Jesus did not conquer.

The highest sacrifice on the highest altar by the highest being has paid the total price for you and the whole world. God accepted the sacrifice, cancelled everything against us and made us part of his body. Any past failure and sins have been judged. These are no more on your record. Fears negate redemption.

## FEARFUL STORMS

### Matt 4:35 -41

*"And the same day, when the even was come, he saith unto them, Let us pass over unto the other side. And when they had sent away the multitude, they took him even as he was in the ship. And there were also with him other little ships. And there arose a great storm of wind, and the waves beat into the ship, so that it was now full. And he was in the hinder part of the ship, asleep on a pillow: and they awake him, and say unto him, Master, carest thou not that we perish? And he arose, and rebuked the wind, and said unto the sea, Peace, be still. And the wind ceased, and there was a great calm. And he said unto them, why are ye so fearful? How is it that ye have no faith? And they feared exceedingly,*

*and said one to another, what manner of man is
this, that even the wind and the sea obey him?"*

Doubt creeps in when you observe all that is
happening around you and forsake the
word of God. Jesus after spending quality
time to teach his disciples about the power
of the word and the operation of the king
told the disciples to go to the other side.

While he was asleep there was a great storm
of hurricane proportion which made the
disciples afraid. They thought they were
dying and darts were being fired at them.
The word they heard from Jesus had
evaporated. They doubted his love for them
and did not speak to the storm. They
observed the ferocity of the storm. No storm
is stronger than the word of God because all
created things were made by the word of
God.

You must take the shield of faith to
effectively use the sword of the spirit. If you

have been hit by a fiery dart because you failed to use your shield, what use is your sword?

On another occasion Peter saw Jesus walking on water and said if it was Jesus he wanted an invitation to join him. The only answer was for Jesus to tell him to come because the request to come walk with Jesus was tied on Jesus identifying himself as the one walking on the water.

He acted on the word of Jesus and began walking towards him but when he observed the effect of the wind he began to sink. The darts were being fired at Peter. It was a miracle that he did not drown at once and Jesus caught him. When people sink it happens at once.

Believers must keep their eyes on the word not the waves and the fiery darts being fired. The shield must go up immediately. The believer needs to immediately use the word as a defence against negative thought pulling down imaginations and things contrary to the word.

Peter already defied natural laws. He did not walk because the sea was quiet. You cannot walk on water on a quiet night, in your river, on the sea neither can it be done in your swimming pool nor your bath tub.

It was the power in the word of Jesus that kept Peter walking. When a new challenge comes, just think back on how the word sustained you in time past – that word is able to sustain you again.

**Matthew 14:24 -32**
*"But the ship was now in the midst of the sea, tossed with waves: for the wind was contrary. And in the fourth watch of the night Jesus went unto them, walking on the sea. And when the disciples saw him walking on the sea, they were troubled, saying, It is a spirit; and they cried out for fear. But straightway Jesus spake unto them,*

*saying, Be of good cheer; it is I; be not afraid. And Peter answered him and said, Lord, if it be thou, bid me come unto thee on the water. And he said, Come. And when Peter was come down out of the ship, he walked on the water, to go to Jesus. But when he saw the wind boisterous, he was afraid; and beginning to sink, he cried, saying, Lord, save me. And immediately Jesus stretched forth his hand, and caught him, and said unto him, O thou of little faith, wherefore didst thou doubt? And when they were come into the ship, the wind ceased."*

## HELMET OF SALVATION & THE SWORD OF THE SPIRIT

The helmet was the last piece of armour the Roman soldier wore. It protected the brain, a very vital organ. This reminds us again that the mind is the battle field. I believe this weapon is a reminder of the progressive renewal of the mind.

There must be a daily application. Believers have areas of their past that they struggle with, hence there needs to be a concentrated effort.

The believer needs to know what he has been saved from, any questions about what Jesus did for you will undoubtedly affect how you use your weapons.

It is non-negotiable. Be sure of what is yours. Satan will negotiate away your redemption if you allow him.

**Eph 6:17**
*"And take the helmet of salvation, and the sword of the Spirit, which is the word of God."*

**Isa 59:17**
*"For he put on righteousness as a breastplate, and an helmet of salvation upon his head; and he put on the garments of vengeance for clothing, and was clad with zeal as a cloak."*

**1Pet 1:13 -**

*"Wherefore gird up the loins of your mind, be sober, and hope to the end for the grace that is to be brought unto you at the revelation of Jesus Christ."*

Experts have said that humans on the average, have 50,000 to 80,000 thoughts daily - 2100 to 3,300 thoughts per hour. This is quite a high traffic.

The Bible teaches that believers should renew their minds with the word.

**Rom 12:1-2**

*"I beseech you therefore, brethren, by the mercies of God, that ye present your bodies a living sacrifice, holy, acceptable unto God, which is your reasonable service. And be not conformed to this world: but be ye transformed by the renewing of your mind, that ye may prove what is that good, and acceptable, and perfect, will of God."*

**Eph 5:26**

*"That he might sanctify and cleanse it with the washing of water by the word."*

**2Cor 10:4**

*"For the weapons of our warfare are not carnal, but mighty through God to the pulling down of strong holds."*

**2Cor 10:5**

*"Casting down imaginations, and every high thing that exalteth itself against the knowledge of God, and bringing into captivity every thought to the obedience of Christ."*

The word 'renew' in verse two also means to renovate, like a building. Places with high traffic like airport toilets are constantly cleaned. The traffic that goes through the mind calls for constant cleaning.

The word for washing in Ephesians 5:26 is the same word for 'a' bath. The more we clean up our minds by casting down imaginations, choosing the thoughts we want to think, casting down those that do not agree with redemption we can be sure our helmet is in place. The believer must reject thoughts that question redemption, thoughts of fear and of sin daily, when this becomes a way of life, this armour is in place. There is no need to ever take the armour off because the enemy is constantly bombarding the minds of believers.

When listening to a radio channel, if you don't like what you hear you tune to another frequency. The same is true for television. You can use the remote control to change channels. Don't let your mind and your body imprison your spirit.

## SWORD OF THE SPIRIT: THE WORD OF GOD

**Eph. 6:17**
*"And take the helmet of salvation, and the sword of the Spirit, which is the word of God."*

The sword of the spirit is using the word of God revealed in your heart against the attacks of the enemy. The believer is expected to wield this sword. The word of God in the heart needs to be expressed through the mouth.

The heart and the mouth are connected. Man believes with the heart, but confession or the release of the faith is through the mouth.

**Rom 10:10**
*"For with the heart man believeth unto righteousness; and with the mouth confession is made unto salvation."*

**Hebrews 4:12-13**
*"For the word of God is quick, and powerful, and sharper than any two-edged sword, piercing even to the dividing asunder of soul and spirit, and of the joints and marrow, and is a discerner of the thoughts and intents of the heart. Neither is there any creature that is not manifest in his sight: but*

*all things are naked and opened unto the eyes of him with whom we have to do."*

What you believe with your heart must be released through the mouth. You cannot wage spiritual warfare with your mouth closed. A natural sword wielded properly is dangerous to the opponent.

The word of God is sharper than a two-edged sword, in the spirit it cuts through all dimensions; spirit, soul, mind, emotions, will, intellect, bone, marrow and the entire body. No creature is immune from its ability. It X-rays, exposes and destroys the works of the enemy in every realm.

The sword of the spirit was used by Jesus when the tempter came to him. Jesus did not try to negotiate or meet the devil on the natural plane. He simply said, 'it is written'. Words from your heart energized by the Holy Spirit, released from your lips will bring God into manifestation. I remembered years ago I went through an hair raising experience. We held a successful outdoor crusade in a small town which provoked the secret cult people.

Many of the people came to faith in Jesus. This event coincided with the season when the witch doctors and masquerades performed a live ritual that required all electricity to be put off as they dragged a live goat sacrifice through the town which had to bleed to death.

I was not acquainted with this tradition so I had lights on and music playing and this attracted them. They felt it was an affront and an insult to them. I heard a commotion nearby and upon opening my window blind, I realized that about seventy persons were chanting and screaming at once.

As I observed closely I realized they were ritualists, witch doctors and masquerades.

They began to chant incantations commanding blindness and death to come upon me.

I felt fear, I began sweating, my heart was racing, but deep down, the word of God from Isaiah 54:17 rose up within me. As I confessed this from a position of despair my confidence rose and the words from my mouth was bolder.

Suddenly, I began to hear thunder and lightning in a dry season. The lightning was localized where the angry mob was and they ran off. The traditional ruler of the community came to check on me the next day and he asked for the secret. I told him it was Jesus. He gave his life to Christ and a large church is in that town today.

The sword of the spirit is the word that has been deposited in your heart and released from your lips in combat. The word must be stored in your heart. The process is confession and meditation. The word of God is spirit and life, a spirit is not limited, it can go through walls and travel great distances. Holy Spirit energized words can cut through space and time bringing deliverance and restoring order.

When Jesus cursed the fig tree, it did not dry up immediately. It began to wither from within. The word will work from the inside to the outside. The fact that there is no immediate result does not mean the word is not working. The centurion told Jesus:

**Mat 8:8**
*"The centurion answered and said, Lord, I am not worthy that thou shouldest come under my roof: but speak the word only, and my servant shall be healed."*

Jesus marvelled because he reminded him of the law in Genesis when God kept speaking and creation exploded. The Holy Spirit is always waiting, brooding and looking out for someone who will speak the word only, so he would have raw material to work with.

## PRACTICE MEDITATING ON THE WORD

A sister who is a teacher, shared how a child in her class had convulsion in the classroom and stopped breathing. She remembered a revelation about the blood and began to plead the blood and the child came around.

An usher in our church had believed for a child for a long time, but at the time of delivery, the child was stillborn. The nurses returned the dead child to the father because the mother had lost so much blood and they were attending to her.

They told him to find a place and bury her. He refused and reminded God how he believed for the child, he and others began to pray and command the child to come back. The girl is alive today and very healthy.

This is not by chance, it is important to spend quality time thinking on scriptures. You may take a scripture in the area you desire results and think on it and apply it personally. Jesus said the house must be built on the rock which is the word of God.

This must happen before the storm. There needs to be a personal relationship with Jesus and his word. The more you read, meditate; mutter the scriptures to yourself over and over again the more faith will come and fear will flee.

The sword of the spirit is effective when the word has been settled in the heart through confession and meditation on the word.

The word meditate in the Hebrew according to Strong's concordance means to 'imagine, meditate, mourn, mutter, roar, sore, speak, study, talk, utter.'

**Joshua 1:8**

*"This book of the law shall not depart out of thy mouth; but thou shalt meditate therein day and night, that thou mayest observe to do according to all that is written therein: for then thou shalt make thy way prosperous, and then thou shalt have good success."*

**Mat 7:24**

*"Therefore, whosoever heareth these sayings of mine, and doeth them, I will liken him unto a wise man, which built his house upon a rock."*

**Mat 7:25**

*"And the rain descended, and the floods came, and the winds blew, and beat upon that house; and it fell not: for it was founded upon a rock."*

David kept releasing his faith in words when he encountered Goliath. His adversary mocked him, but he kept saying what he believed. The woman with the issue of blood heard about Jesus but she kept saying what she believed. Faith that says nothing and believes nothing receives nothing. What is believed must be followed by corresponding action and God will honour his word.

I read the other day about a certain prophet who said his own words are superior to God's word. No prophet's word is superior to the word of God. God upholds all things by the word of his power. (Hebrews 1:3).

These sorts of Prophets make simple minded believers believe that all they need in their life is a prophet not a relationship with Jesus. The word that will bring deliverance in time of trouble is the one digested.

Natural food must be processed by digestion before the energy is released into the body. You need time in the word. God is raising an elite army who is not running after the 'so-called prophets,' but have a thriving relationship with the Lord Jesus.

# Chapter six

## TYPES OF PRAYERS

**Eph. 6:18**
*"Praying always with all prayer and supplication in the Spirit, and watching thereunto with all perseverance and supplication for all saints."*

It is very important that we understand that there are different types of prayer as we wage warfare and keep our armour on. Different rules guide the different types of prayers. There are different types of sports but what is lawful in one sport, may attract a penalty in another. Soccer players use their feet, apart from the goalkeeper who may use his hands and feet as the condition applies, but basketball is different, you are not allowed to use your feet at all.

This is one reason many prayers go unanswered because the believer is breaching the rules. We may group the prayers into the following groups:

Prayer of petition or the prayer of faith. In order to pray the prayer of petition, you need to know and establish the will of God. There can be no faith where the will of God is unknown.

You cannot believe beyond the knowledge you have. Supposing you want to make a request to a bank for a loan, you would need to establish and know for sure if the bank offers such services. The prayer of the petition must be a prayer of faith. It primarily concerns your individual desires, needs, and problems. It is you praying for yourself, not someone else praying for you or agreeing with you in prayer.

There are no ifs' in the prayer of petition, the will of God is clear, for example, salvation of loved ones, healing, forgiveness, provision, protection; the will of God is clear. You also need to have scriptures that cover that.

The prayer of petition must be done in faith and concluded in thanksgiving. In the prayer of faith, you receive when you pray. Once done in faith, this prayer does not need to be repeated.

There is no use praying for God to give you another man's car, house or wife because there are no promises and scriptures where you are promised those things.

**John 15:16**
*"Ye have not chosen me, but I have chosen you, and ordained you, that ye should go and bring forth fruit, and that your fruit should remain that*

*whatsoever ye shall ask of the Father in my name, he may give it you."*

## John 15:7
*"If ye abide in me, and my words abide in you, ye shall ask what ye will and it shall be done unto you."*

## Matt.7:7 -11
*"Ask and it shall be given you; seek, and ye shall find, knock and it shall be opened unto you: For every one that asketh received and he that seeketh findeth and to him that knocketh it shall be opened. Or what man is there of you, whom if his son ask bread, will he give him a stone? Or if he ask a fish, will he give him a serpent? If ye then, being evil, know how to give good gifts unto your children, how much more shall your Father which is in heaven give good things to them that ask him?"*

## 1John 5:14
*"And this is the confidence that we have in him, that, if we ask any thing according to his will, he*

*heareth us."*

## Mark 11:24-24

*"Therefore, I say unto you, What things soever ye desire, when ye pray, believe that ye receive them, and ye shall have them."*

## James 5:14

*"Is any sick among you? Let him call for the elders of the church; and let them pray over him, anointing him with oil in the name of the Lord."*

## James 5:15

*"And the prayer of faith shall save the sick, and the Lord shall raise him up and if he has committed sins, they shall be forgiven him."*

## PRAYER OF CONSECRATION OR DEDICATION

Jesus prayed the prayer of consecration when he dedicated himself to go to the cross. The prayer of dedication is used when the will of God is unknown or you desire to fulfil the will of God in the face of apparent challenges. The prayer of faith cannot be repeated but the prayer of dedication can be repeated.

Jesus prayed the prayer of dedication three times. The garden of Gethsemane was the place where Jesus accepted the cup of wrath, before this time, he was untouchable. He sweated blood as he wrestled in prayer, but he submitted to the will of the father.

When praying about whom to marry, where to go to church, where to work, where to live, things that are not spelt out in the Bible like salvation of love ones and bodily healing you need to pray the prayer of consecration or dedication as often as you need it.

It is a way of saying to the Lord, not my will but thy will be done. It is recognizing him as the porter and yourself as the clay. It is important that you are committed to doing the will of God when it is revealed. It is a prayer that lays your all on the altar.

## Matthew 26:36-44

*"Then cometh Jesus with them unto a place called Gethsemane, and saith unto the disciples, Sit ye here, while I go and pray yonder. And he took with him Peter and the two sons of Zebedee, and began to be sorrowful and very heavy Then saith he unto them, My soul is exceeding sorrowful, even unto death: tarry ye here, and watch with me. And he went a little further, and fell on his face, and prayed, saying, O my Father, if it be possible, let this cup pass from me: nevertheless not as I will but as thou wilt. And he cometh unto the disciples, and findeth them asleep and sat unto Peter, What, could ye not watch with me one hour? Watch and pray, that ye enter not into temptation: the spirit indeed is willing, but the flesh is weak. He went away again the second time, and prayed, saying, O my Father, if this cup may not pass away from me, except I drink it, thy will be done. And he came and found them asleep again: for their eyes were heavy. And he*

*left them, and went away again, and prayed the third time, saying the same words."*

## Mark 14: 34-40

*"And saith unto them, My soul is exceeding sorrowful unto death: tarry ye here, and watch And he went forward a little, and fell on the ground, and prayed that, if it were possible, the hour might pass from him. And he said, Abba, Father, all things are possible unto thee; take away this cup from me: nevertheless not what I will but what thou wilt. And he cometh, and findeth them sleeping and saith unto Peter, Simon, sleepest thou couldest not thou watch one hour? Watch ye and pray, lest ye enter into temptation. The spirit truly is ready, but the flesh is weak. And again he went away and prayed and spake the same words. And when he returned, he found them asleep again, (for their eyes were heavy neither wist they what to answer."*

## PRAYER OF CASTING YOUR CARE

Peter wrote about casting our cares on the Lord and he is a great example of one who did that.

Herod was going to have his head cut off the next day, yet he slept so soundly that the angel had to smite him to get up. How many people will be facing execution from a paramount dictator and sleep soundly?

Peter had committed the situation into the hands of God and knew God was working on it. If we rewind his life backwards, we find Peter not being directly threatened, when they came to arrest Jesus, but he took his sword and took off the ear of Marcus, the servant high Priest.

When cares are given to the Lord, it means you no longer have it, talking, thinking and reminiscing over the situation is taking it back. The peace of God that passes all understanding is a fruit of casting cares on the Lord.

If there are anxieties, worries and concerns, then the care has not been given to God. The command to worry is not a suggestion nor an advice.

**1 Peter 5:7 AMPC**

*"Casting the whole of your care [all your anxieties, all your worries, all your concerns, once and for all] on Him, for He cares for you affectionately and cares about you watchfully."*

**Philippians 4:6-7 AMPC**

*"Do not fret or have any anxiety about anything, but in every circumstance and in everything, by prayer and petition definite requests, with thanksgiving, continue to make your wants known to God. And God's peace [shall be yours, that tranquil state of a soul assured of its salvation through Christ, and so fearing nothing from God and being content with its earthly lot, of whatever sort, that is, that peace] which*

*transcends all understanding shall garrison and mount guard over your hearts and minds in Christ Jesus."*

## Act 12:1-10

*"Now about that time Herod the king stretched forth his hands to vex certain of the church. And he killed James the brother of John with the sword. And because he saw it pleased the Jews, he proceeded further to take Peter also. (Then were the days of unleavened bread.) And when he had apprehended him, he put him in prison, and delivered him to four quaternions of soldiers to keep him; intending after Easter to bring him forth to the people. Peter therefore was kept in prison: but prayer was made without ceasing of the church unto God for him. And when Herod would have brought him forth, the same night Peter was sleeping between two soldiers, bound with two chains: and the keepers before the door kept the prison. And, behold, the angel of the Lord came upon him, and a light shined in the prison: and he smote Peter on the side, and raised him up, saying, Arise up quickly. And his chains fell*

*off from his hands. And the angel said unto him, Gird thyself, and bind on thy sandals. And so he did. And he saith unto him, Cast thy garment about thee, and follow me. And he went out, and followed him; and wist not that it was true which was done by the angel; but thought he saw a vision. When they were past the first and the second ward, they came unto the iron gate that leadeth unto the city; which opened to them of his own accord: and they went out, and passed on through one street; and forthwith the angel departed from him."*

A woman from a remote village was carrying luggage on her head when she flagged a car down for a ride. On getting in she refused to put her load down concerned she would add more weight to the vehicle.

Jesus wants to be your burden bearer, release the weight of it. He is able. The birds and the flowers in the analogy that Jesus gave in Matthew 6 from verse 25 are carefree because our Heavenly Father looks after them. God wants his children to be carefree because they are more important than birds and the very hair on the believer's head is numbered.

## Matthew 6:25 -33

*Therefore I say unto you, Take no thought for your life, what ye shall eat, or what ye shall drink, nor yet for your body, what ye shall put on Is not the life more than meat, and the body than raiment? Behold the fowls of the air: for they sow not, neither do they reap, nor gather into barns; yet your heavenly Father feedeth them. Are ye not much better than they? Which of you by taking thought can add one cubit unto his stature? And why take ye thought for raiment? Consider the lilies of the field, how they grow, they toil not, neither do they spin. And yet I say unto you, That even Solomon in all his glory was not arrayed like one of these. Wherefore, if God so clothe the grass of the field, which to day is, and to morrow is cast into the oven, shall he not much more clothe you, O ye of little faith? Therefore take no thought, saying, What shall we eat or,*

*What shall we drink or, Wherewithal shall we be clothed. (For after all these things do the Gentiles seek for your heavenly Father knoweth that ye have need of all these things. But seek ye first the kingdom of God, and his righteousness; and all these things shall be added unto you. Take therefore no thought for the morrow: for the morrow shall take thought for the things of itself. Sufficient unto the day is the evil thereof."*

## PRAYER OF BINDING & LOOSING / PRAYER OF AGREEMENT

### Mat 18:18 -20

*"Verily I say unto you, Whatsoever ye shall bind on earth shall be bound in heaven: and whatsoever ye shall loose on earth shall be loosed in heaven. Again' I say unto you, That if two of you shall agree on earth as touching anything that they shall ask, it shall be done for them of my Father which is in heaven. For where two or three are gathered together in my name, there am I in the midst of them."*

The prayer of agreement must be done in faith. If you propose an agreement on a contract for a house you'll sit down to write out the terms. There is a need to know exactly what you are agreeing on and the scriptures you are presenting to heaven to back your agreement.

The agreement on earth should be in agreement with what obtains in heaven. There is no sickness there so if you want heaven's backing you must tailor your agreement with what obtains in heaven.

The power of agreement starts here on earth because God gave man dominion on the earth. What the first Adam lost the second Adam, Jesus, restored.

As God's representatives on the earth, believers are called to rule and reign with the backing of heaven. God always needs a man on the earth to establish his will. Jesus is the head and we are the body. The church has the authority to bind demonic spirits on the earth and heaven will back the church up. The church can also loose the ministry of angels on the earth and heaven will give the backing.

A couple can use the force of agreement because they are already joined together in marriage. When any believer uses the prayer of agreement, make sure there is agreement in word and in spirit.

THE PRAYER OF MINISTERING UNTO THE LORD OR PRAYER OF THANKSGIVING

A distinctive feature of this prayer is that you are not really asking for anything. You are just worshiping, communing with the Lord and giving him thanks.

Paul and Silas were flogged and cast into prison with their backs bleeding, they were not arguing and wondering why they were there, but they cast their cares on the Lord and actually burst into praise. This sort of praise is a sacrifice which qualifies for a reply from heaven and absolutely confuses the devil.

Suddenly, there was an earthquake and their bounds were loose. They sang praises to God in the most difficult time of their life. They were simply enjoying God and the prisoners heard them, I'm sure they thought they were crazy.

Praise and thanksgiving should be part of every prayer, it shows a rest that the matter is settled. What Paul wrote about prayer in Philippians 4:6 was born out of experience. They prayed with Silas, nothing happened, but when they began to praise God an earthquake showed up.

**Acts 16: 23-26**
*"And when they had laid many stripes upon them, they cast them into prison, charging the*

*jailor to keep them safely: Who, having received such a charge, thrust them into the inner prison, and made their feet fast in the stocks. And at midnight Paul and Silas prayed and sang praises unto God: and the prisoners heard them. And suddenly there was a great earthquake, so that the foundations of the prison were shaken and immediately all the doors were opened and every one's bands were loosed."*

### Philippians 4:6

*"Be careful for nothing; but in everything by prayer and supplication with thanksgiving let your requests be made known unto God."*

### Philippians 4:7

*"And the peace of God, which passeth all understanding, shall keep your hearts and minds through Christ Jesus."*

### Acts 13:1

*"Now there were in the church that was at Antioch certain prophets and teachers; as Barnabas, and Simeon that was called Niger, and*

*Lucius of Cyrene, and Manaen, which had been brought up with Herod the tetrarch, and Saul."*

### Acts 13:2
*"As they ministered to the Lord, and fasted the Holy Ghost said, Separate me Barnabas and Saul for the work whereunto I have called them."*

Some prophets and teachers had gathered at Antioch not to make a request but to minister to the Lord. God indwells the worship of his people. They were just enjoying God when God told them to separate Paul and Barnabas for the work he had called them.

This worship atmosphere is needed for the Holy Spirit to minister. I remember many years ago, a few of us gathered just to minister to the Lord, as I looked up, I saw a cloud descend into the room.

This white cloud brought in an awesome presence of God. As the cloud touched each person's head they went to the floor in slow motion. Many secrets of the Holy Spirit were revealed on that day.

# Chapter Seven

## TYPES OF PRAYERS II
## PRAYER OF INTERCESSION

The prayer of intercession is a prayer we are called to pray as believers. A person who prays the prayer of intercession is standing in the gap to avert judgment, to change things on behalf of others.

Generally, this prayer is a prayer for others. There are accounts of intercession in the Bible, we shall look at a few examples to learn the principle.

The world is moving fast with a jet and a micro wave mentality, people want answers to prayer before their request is made. Unfortunately, the prayer of intercession is not an instant prayer. It takes time and maybe days, it requires diligence and sacrifice.

This type of prayer is needed more today because there are spiritual warfares over the nations, the body of Christ, loved ones and for revival. God is calling more believes to be sensitive when he nudges us to intercede.

ABRAHAM'S INTERCESSION

God said he was not going to do anything without telling Abraham his friend. We as believers are in covenant with God just like Abraham was.

When God reveals something bad or negative, it is not for believers to just discuss it glibly, but it is a call for prayer. Abraham negotiated down to ten persons, he must have imagined that Lot ought to have up to ten righteous persons in his household. It is the responsibility of the church when judgment is revealed to intercede against it.

God will hold the church in each area responsible for what they allow to happen. Adam was the god of the earth. We are called to rule and reign on the earth as the body of Christ. Many unfortunate things have happened which are called by the secular world the acts of God because the believers did not step in to cancel or abort the works of the enemy.

Your blood covenant relationship through Christ means that you are the family of God, His representative on the earth, he must run things by you where your family and nation is concerned. Abraham was so bold he challenged God to do right.

His audacity and boldness was based on oneness through covenant. He was God's man and ambassador to the earth. What a privilege and what authority God has given to believers by virtue of the covenant through the blood of Jesus.

**Genesis 18: 23 -33**

*"And Abraham drew near and said Wilt thou also destroy the righteous with the wicked? Peradventure there be fifty righteous within the city: wilt thou also destroy and not spare the place for the fifty righteous that are therein? That be far from thee to do after this manner, to slay the righteous with the wicked: and that the righteous should be as the wicked, that be far from thee: Shall not the Judge of all the earth do right? And the LORD said If I find in Sodom fifty righteous within the city, then I will spare all the place for their sakes. And Abraham answered and said Behold now, I have taken upon me to speak unto the Lord, which am but dust and ashes: Peradventure there shall lack five of the fifty righteous: wilt thou destroy all the city for lack of*

*five? And he said If I find there forty and five, I will not destroy it. And he spake unto him yet again and said Peradventure there shall be forty found there. And he said I will not do it for forty's sake. And he said unto him, Oh let not the Lord be angry and I will speak Peradventure there shall thirty be found there. And he said I will not do it, if I find thirty there. And he said Behold now, I have taken upon me to speak unto the Lord: Peradventure there shall be twenty found there. And he said I will not destroy it for twenty's sake. And he said Oh let not the Lord be angry and I will speak yet but this once: Peradventure ten shall be found there. And he said I will not destroy it for ten's sake. And the LORD went his way as soon as he had left communing with Abraham: and Abraham returned unto his place."*

## DANIEL'S INTERCESSION

### Daniel 10: 1-3,11-13

*"In the third year of Cyrus king of Persia a thing was revealed unto Daniel, whose name was called*

*Belteshazzar; and the thing was true, but the time appointed was long: and he understood the thing, and had understanding of the vision. In those days I Daniel was mourning three full weeks. I ate no pleasant bread, neither came flesh nor wine in my mouth, neither did I anoint myself at all till three whole weeks were fulfilled.*

Daniel 10:11-13

*"And he said unto me, O Daniel, a man greatly beloved, understand the words that I speak unto thee, and stand upright: for unto thee am I now sent And when he had spoken this word unto me, I stood trembling. Then said he unto me, Fear not, Daniel: for from the first day that thou didst set thine heart to understand and to chasten thyself before thy God, thy words were heard and I am come for thy words.. But the prince of the kingdom of Persia withstood me one and twenty days: but, lo, Michael, one of the chief princes, came to help me; and I remained there with the kings of Persia."*

Daniel received a revelation for which he needed clarity and he waited on the Lord in fasting for three weeks. The angel finally comes with the answer following the detail and explained to Daniel that his prayer was heard on the first day but he had resistance in the spirit realm from a demonic spiritual ruler who bore the same name as the kingdom Persia where Daniel lived at the time. God had to send Michael down for reinforcement before his answer could come through.

The prophet Ezekiel, writing about the physical kingdom of Tyrus also mentioned the demonic kingdom. There is a dual kingdom or system everywhere in the world.

Satan tried to undermine the system of God, he copies everything, but he has been defeated and the authority has been released to the church to dominate him in the spirit. One of the weapons of warfare is the prayer of intercession when the believer is enabled by the Holy Spirit to pull down strongholds of the enemy.

Unsaved people cannot exercise dominion in the realm of the Spirit because they have no qualification to enter into such a fight. The blood of Jesus is the identity that places the believer at an advantage in spiritual warfare. The indwelling Holy Spirit helps the believer to be successful in prayer.

### Ezekiel 28:12 -19

*"Son of man, take up a lamentation upon the king of Tyrus, and say unto him, Thus saith the Lord GOD; Thou sealest up the sum, full of wisdom, and perfect in beauty. Thou hast been in Eden the garden of God; every precious stone was thy covering, the sardius, topaz, and the diamond, the beryl, the onyx, and the jasper, the sapphire, the emerald, and the carbuncle, and gold: the workmanship of thy tabrets and of thy pipes was prepared in thee in the day that thou wast created. Thou art the anointed cherub that covereth and I have set thee so: thou wast upon*

*the holy mountain of God; thou hast walked up and down in the midst of the stones of fire. Thou wast perfect in thy ways from the day that thou wast created till iniquity was found in thee. By the multitude of thy merchandise they have filled the midst of thee with violence, and thou hast sinned therefore I will cast thee as profane out of the mountain of God: and I will destroy thee, O covering cherub, from the midst of the stones of fire. Thine heart was lifted up because of thy beauty, thou hast corrupted thy wisdom by reason of thy brightness: I will cast thee to the ground, I will lay thee before kings, that they may behold thee. Thou hast defiled thy sanctuaries by the multitude of thine iniquities, by the iniquity of thy traffick; therefore will I bring forth a fire from the midst of thee, it shall devour thee, and I will bring thee to ashes upon the earth in the sight of all them that behold thee. All they that know thee among the people shall be astonished at thee: thou shalt be a terror, and never shalt thou be any more."*

**Eph. 6:12**

*"For we wrestle not against flesh and blood, but against principalities, against powers, against the rulers of the darkness of this world, against spiritual wickedness in high places."*

PRAYERS FOR THOSE IN AUTHORITY

**1 Timothy 2:1-3**

*"I exhort therefore, that, first of all, supplications, prayers, intercessions, and giving of thanks, be made for all men; For kings and for all that are in authority; that we may lead a quiet and peaceable life in all godliness and honesty. For this is good and acceptable in the sight of God our Saviour."*

Paul exhorts that prayer should be made for those in authority, these were mainly despotic leaders of the day who persecuted the church.

Praying for them will reduce the amount of demonic activity around them, we can

control governments from our knees. We
need to be reminded that at the time of
Paul's writing their wicked leaders fed
Christians to lion's and persecuted the
church beyond measure, but he believed
interceding for them would control how
much they yielded to the demonic realm.

Truly, the believers are the watchmen. They
have authority in three worlds; Heaven,
earth and hell. This authority cannot be
contested. Believers are therefore spiritually
positioned to undo the works of the enemy.
The spiritual controls the natural, once
believers can destroy the root of an attack in
the spirit, the manifestation in the natural
will be aborted.

## PRAYING WITH THE HELP OF THE HOLY SPIRIT

The baptism of the Holy Spirit and the
prayer language that follows is a powerful
investment from heaven. When the believer

prays in tongues, his human spirit energized by the Holy Spirit is making direct uninterrupted contact with heaven. The believer is praying the will of God because the Holy Spirit knows the will of God. The believer is able to tap into the abundance of God's wisdom to pray accurately.

GROANING IN THE SPIRIT

There are times during intercession, that the Holy Spirit begins to give groaning to the believer. Isaiah likens groaning to a woman in labour. A woman in labour groans because she is about to have a baby. She is carrying a burden so to speak and she labours to bring the baby forth. Similarly, when prayer becomes groaning the believer must pray until that burden is expressed.

I believe many of the evil things happening today are taking place because the church has drawn back from intercession with groaning because of the excesses of the past.

What would happen to any woman who refuses labour in her pregnancy the baby will not be born or she would settle for a Cesarean section. A burden must be fully expressed, just like labour time for women differs, the amount of time spent in prayers, when you are burdened by the Lord depends on the Holy Spirit. It could be days, hours, minutes, but yield to God.

As watchmen over families, churches, cities and nations, praying in the Holy Spirit with groaning should be embraced. A few minutes can save a life. The enemy wants to inflict maximum pain on people, but the church can stop him by standing in the gap and making up the hedge. As believers allow the Holy Spirit to pray through them, he knows where the danger is, he knows the right words to pray using the believer's lips.

**Isa 66:7 -9**
*"Before she travailed, she brought forth; before her pain came, she was delivered of a man child.*

*Who hath heard such a thing? who hath seen such things? Shall the earth be made to bring forth in one day? or shall a nation be born at once? for as soon as Zion travailed, she brought forth her children. Shall I bring to the birth, and not cause to bring forth? saith the LORD: shall I cause to bring forth, and shut the womb? saith thy God."*

**Dan 4:17**
*"This matter is by the decree of the watchers, and the demand by the word of the holy ones: to the intent that the living may know that the most High ruleth in the kingdom of men, and giveth it to whomsoever he will, and setteth up over it the basest of men."*

INTERCESSION AND REMOVAL OF KINGS

**Ezekiel 22:30**
*"And I sought for a man among them, that should make up the hedge, and stand in the gap*

*before me for the land, that I should not destroy it: but I found none."*

**Ezekiel 22:31**
*"Therefore have I poured out mine indignation upon them; I have consumed them with the fire of my wrath: their own way have I recompensed upon their heads, saith the Lord GOD. "*

ELIJAH'S INTERCESSION

Elijah under the old covenant, told Ahab to eat and drink because he heard the sound of rain in the spirit but there was no cloud in sight. He took the position of intercession in those days and prayed until rain came after three and half years.

There are events that God has planned, but he is waiting for believers to birth them in the Spirit. There was nothing at the start of his prayer. Zero. He kept praying and the servant came back it was after the sixth time, at the seventh time that he saw cloud size of a man's hand. He told Ahab to get into his chariot. Spiritual victories, fights over destines are won in the spirit before they manifest in the natural.

## 1Kings18:41-46

*"And Elijah said unto Ahab, Get thee up, eat and drink; for there is a sound of abundance of rain. So Ahab went up to eat and to drink. And Elijah went up to the top of Carmel; and he cast himself down upon the earth, and put his face between his knees, And said to his servant, Go up now, look toward the sea. And he went up, and looked, and said, There is nothing. And he said, Go again seven times. And it came to pass at the seventh time, that he said, Behold, there ariseth a little cloud out of the sea, like a man's hand. And he said, Go up, say unto Ahab, Prepare thy chariot, and get thee down, that the rain stop thee not. And it came to pass in the mean while, that the heaven was black with clouds and wind, and there was a great rain. And Ahab rode, and went to Jezreel. And the hand of the LORD was on*

*Elijah; and he girded up his loins, and ran before Ahab to the entrance of Jezreel."*

### James 5:16 AMPC

*"Confess to one another therefore your faults (your slips, your false steps, your offenses, your sins) and pray [also] for one another, that you may be healed and restored [to a spiritual tone of mind and heart]. The earnest (heartfelt, continued) prayer of a righteous man makes tremendous power available [dynamic in its working."*

Intercessory prayers with groaning can be passionate and may be outright offensive to some. Women do not travail in public, find a quiet spot and win your victories.

Those who are ashamed of this type of prayer will have to run on the energy of the flesh. This type of intercession will do more in an hour than many months of human effort.

**Galatians 4:19**

*"My little children, of whom I travail in birth again until Christ be formed in you."*

**Romans 8:26**

*"Likewise the Spirit also helpeth our infirmities: for we know not what we should pray for as we ought, but the Spirit itself maketh intercession for us with groanings which cannot be uttered."*

Paul in his letter to the Ephesians said he travails before they were saved and is doing it again for them to be established in the faith. Many times, there is a harvest of souls, but soon the harvest disappears.

There is a need to travail when the spirit leads in this way for new believers. There are demonic activities set up to derail them from the path they have chosen.

In the spirit, intercession can ward off those demonic influences and God can order their steps and bring them into maturity.

## INTERCESSION RELEASES ANGELS OF DELIVERANCE AND JUDGEMENT

As the church interceded for the release of Peter, God sent an angel. When prayer is made in the Holy Spirit, there are revelations that are released in prayer that the mind may not understand.

It is not a coincidence that Peter was released by an angel and Herod was smitten by an angel. The angel struck Peter and he was released from prison and the angel struck Herod, a powerful paramount ruler and he was eaten by worms.

Herod put to death those in charge of the prison because he could not get Peter. He thought Peter had escaped yet there was no jail break.

The sequence of events showed that had the church not prayed without ceasing, Peter would have also died like James the brother of John, whom Herod killed with the sword. Where our affairs on earth are concerned, God will never move out of turn. The earth had been given to us to rule and reign.

As the early church prayed, God allowed an angel to strike Herod and he was eaten of worms, thereafter the word of God grew and multiplied. It came by reason of judgment.

Acts 12:1-7
*"Now about that time Herod the king stretched forth his hands to vex certain of the church. And he killed James the brother of John with the sword. And because he saw it pleased the Jews, he proceeded further to take Peter also. (Then were the days of unleavened bread.) And when he had apprehended him, he put him in prison, and delivered him to four quaternions of soldiers to keep him; intending after Easter to bring him forth to the people. Peter therefore was kept in prison: but prayer was made without ceasing of the church unto God for him. And when Herod*

*would have brought him forth, the same night Peter was sleeping between two soldiers, bound with two chains: and the keepers before the door kept the prison. And, behold, the angel of the Lord came upon him, and a light shined in the prison: and he smote Peter on the side, and raised him up, saying, Arise up quickly. And his chains fell off from his hands."*

**2Thess.1:6**

*"Seeing it is a righteous thing with God to recompense tribulation to them that trouble you."*

**Act 12:19 -24**

*"And when Herod had sought for him, and found him not, he examined the keepers, and commanded that they should be put to death. And he went down from Judaea to Caesarea, and there abode. And Herod was highly displeased with them of Tyre and Sidon: but they came with one accord to him, and, having made Blastus the king's chamberlain their friend, desired peace; because their country was nourished by the*

*king's country. And upon a set day Herod, arrayed in royal apparel, sat upon his throne, and made an oration unto them. And the people gave a shout, saying, It is the voice of a god, and not of a man. And immediately the angel of the Lord smote him, because he gave not God the glory: and he was eaten of worms, and gave up the ghost. But the word of God grew and multiplied."*

There will be times when the spirit of God may lead believers to declare judgment on wicked leaders in the spirit. When it is done by the Holy Spirit, God will see to it that it comes to pass. Some leaders may need to be removed for the word to grow and multiply.

# Chapter Eight

# EAGLE BELIEVER

**Deuteronomy 32:10-14 MSG**

*"He found him out in the wilderness, in an empty, windswept wasteland. He threw his arms around him, lavished attention on him, guarding him as the apple of his eye. He was like an eagle hovering over its nest, overshadowing its young, Then spreading its wings, lifting them into the air, teaching them to fly. GOD alone led him; there was not a foreign god in sight. GOD lifted him onto the hilltops, so he could feast on the crops in the fields. He fed him honey from the rock, oil from granite crags, Curds of cattle and the milk of sheep, the choice cuts of lambs and*

*goats, Fine Bashan rams, high-quality wheat, and the blood of grapes: you drank good wine!"*

**Isa 40:28 -31**

*"Hast thou not known? hast thou not heard, that the everlasting God, the LORD, the Creator of the ends of the earth, fainteth not, neither is weary? there is no searching of his understanding. He giveth power to the faint; and to them that have no might he increaseth strength. Even the youths shall faint and be weary, and the young men shall utterly fall: But they that wait upon the LORD shall renew their strength; they shall mount up with wings as eagles; they shall run, and not be weary; and they shall walk, and not faint. "*

STIRRING INTO DESTINY

The eagle is the believer ideally considered, God likens himself to the mother eagle. Eagles are majestic birds with microscopic and telescopic eyesight, they see far and near. The eagle and her mate nest very high to prevent predators getting to the nest.

They may use a high hill, mountain, or tall trees as places to build their nest.

They use sharp sticks, thorns in the outer part of the nest as these will keep predators away, on the inside of the nest they use rags, animal skin and their own soft feathers to make it super comfortable for the eaglet.

Both male and female eagles bring food, choice meat and delicacies. The eaglet is super comfortable in the nest and is content to stay in this place of safety. After a while the mother Eagle decides it's time for the eagle to experience the blue sky and prepare for life in the wild.

**Deut 32:10 -12**
*"He found him in a desert land, and in the waste howling wilderness; he led him about, he instructed him, he kept him as the apple of his eye. As an eagle stirreth up her nest, fluttereth over her young, spreadeth abroad her wings, taketh them, beareth them on her wings: So the*

*LORD alone did lead him, and there was no strange god with him."*

The stirring of the nest is the season when the eagle must get out of the nest. The mother Eagle begins to remove all the soft materials used for the inside of the nest, the feathers, rags, animal skin are removed and the eaglet is sitting on sharp sticks and is very uncomfortable.

When it's time for the next level of spiritual growth, God allows the believer to come into an uncomfortable season.

The children of Israel had choice land in Goshen for many years until another Pharaoh that did not know Joseph arose. He killed their children and oppressed them as slaves until they began to cry to God. It was also a time for them to go into the land of promise.

God is not the author of sickness, oppression and wickedness but he would use whatever the devil throws at the believer as a stepping stone to move closer to his purpose and destiny.

God stirs your nest to release you into destiny. To stir in Hebrew is to make bare, when God makes things bare, where you were satisfied no longer satisfies, there is a deeper hunger for more. In the season of shaking God is more interested in your character than your comfort.

The believer is not created for the nest. In the nest, you cannot spread your wings and you cannot soar. Everything the eaglet needs to succeed she possesses apart from practice.

Terah, Abraham's Father received the instruction to go to Canaan but he stopped in Haran and God had to call Abraham after his death. A place where we stay within our comfort zone will hinder destiny. The sticks and materials used for the eagle's nest are a reflection of where her parents have been. In our spiritual growth things that are part of our family or church heritage that are not scriptural have to be removed or shaken.

Moses' world was shaken again when God told him to return to Egypt after forty years. He had settled in Midian into a quiet life but God wanted him to fulfil a purpose. He wanted him out of his place of comfort after forty years.

Peter was told to launch deeper into the sea, but he was not ready for this. The Sea of Galilee was 200 meters below sea level, people did not fish that deep because the sea was subject to violent storms. Peter did and it changed him.

The mother Eagle stirs the nest, makes it bare, just to make the eaglet uncomfortable enough to want to leave the nest. People generally see the world through the prism of the nest they are born into. The eaglets who handled money the way their fathers and mothers handled money may be very shaken when God moves in their life.

There could be other areas like ministry, marriage, work, children, but when it's time to go to another level, God is always more interested in your character than your comfort.

## Genesis 11:31; 12:3

*"And Terah took Abram his son, and Lot the son of Haran his son's son, and Sarai his daughter in law, his son Abram's wife; and they went forth with them from Ur of the Chaldees, to go into the land of Canaan; and they came unto Haran, and dwelt there. And the days of Terah were two hundred and five years: and Terah died in Haran."*

## Genesis 12:3

*"Now the Lord had said unto Abram, Get thee out of thy country, and from thy kindred, and*

*from thy father's house, unto a land that I will shew thee: And I will make of thee a great nation, and I will bless thee, and make thy name great; and thou shalt be a blessing: And I will bless them that bless thee, and curse him that curseth thee:and in thee shall all families of the earth be blessed."*

## Luke 5:4 -8

*"Now when he had left speaking, he said unto Simon, Launch out into the deep, and let down your nets for a draught. And Simon answering said unto him, Master, we have toiled all the night, and have taken nothing: nevertheless at thy word I will let down the net. And when they had this done, they inclosed a great multitude of fishes: and their net brake. And they beckoned unto their partners, which were in the other ship, that they should come and help them. And they came, and filled both the ships, so that they began to sink. When Simon Peter saw it, he fell down at Jesus' knees, saying, Depart from me; for I am a sinful man, O Lord."*

## FLUTTERING AND SPREADING OF WINGS

The next thing the mother eagle does is to flutter her wings. She lifts up and spreads her wings over the young. This is a show of strength and reassurance by the mother eagle. She wants the eaglet to know even though she is uncomfortable sitting on sticks and hanging dangerously on a cliff edge she is covered.

The spread of a mother eagle's wing is between 7 to 8 feet. The eaglets do not know her mother's wings were that big.

**Psalm 105:27**
*"They shewed his signs among them, and wonders in the land of Ham."*

God showed Israel many miracles as he brought them out of Egypt. There was a supernatural force field around them and the plagues could not get to Goshen. Israel was no longer comfortable in Egypt, but had a struggle with leaving the known for the unknown. The great commission will never be fulfilled by sitting in the nest.

The church must leave her comfort zone. The eaglet has been looking at the blue skies but it is now time to experience why she was born. She was born to be free, to experience the wild, so the props have to go.

The same is true of the believer, God will stir the nest, so we can fulfil destiny. Jesus allowed his disciples to face a storm while he slept, he wanted them to learn to use their authority instead they blamed him for not caring.

The mother eagle nudges the eaglet to the edge of the cliff and she lays one of the wings down as an invitation to the eaglet to get off the sharp stick ends on which she is perching dangerously. The eaglet is facing eviction, she must fly or die.

The eaglet accepts the mother eagle's invite, gets on the wings and the mother eagle takes her on an adventure of a lifetime in the blue sky. Exhilarating, beautiful ride, now she makes the rational choice of not perching dangerously on stick ends, and chooses to ride with the mother.

She is in her elements in the sky, she was born to be free. There is more to come as the mother does a somersault and dumps the eaglet she is falling fast at great speed and she is sure this definitely is her end. Her life flashes before her, she remembers the comfort of her nest and wonders why she agreed on this dangerous adventure.

As she prepares for the worst, saying her last prayers, the mother eagle picks her up, she is so relieved and is encouraged that her mother cares. This happens more times till she realizes she too has a pair of wings, she begins to flap them and soon is flying like the mother. Other skill sets needed for survival in the wild are taught to her. She is trained to set her wings, which allows her to mount up against the storm.

TRAINING FOR REIGNING

The believer, like the eaglet must learn to confront her fears, the fear of the unknown, the fear of leaving the nest. Jesus has sent the church as sheep among wolves, He believes the church is strong enough to confront wolves. Whatever you fear controls you. God did not raise up the church with Jesus to be afraid of the enemy.

The three Hebrew children refused to fear the fiery furnace, and it could not consume them. The early church prayed for boldness as they confronted the political leadership that wanted them dead.

You were recreated to overcome storms. The same spirit that raised Jesus from the dead is in the believer. Jesus has already overcome all the forces of hell put together in their domain energized by the same Holy Spirit living within the believer.

You are more than a conqueror because Jesus defeated the devil for you. He gave you his victory, and left the Holy Spirit within you to help you in every crisis of life. The storms that destroy others is another opportunity for muscle building, another opportunity to soar and mount up with wings.

**1Jn 4:4**
*"Ye are of God, little children, and have overcome them: because greater is he that is in you, than he that is in the world."*

**2Cor 4:7 -10**
*"But we have this treasure in earthen vessels, that the excellency of the power may be of God, and not of us. We are troubled on every side, yet not distressed; we are perplexed, but not in despair; Persecuted, but not forsaken; cast down, but not destroyed; Always bearing about in the*

*body the dying of the Lord Jesus, that the life also of Jesus might be made manifest in our body."*

## 1 Peter 2:9-10

*"But ye are a chosen generation, a royal priesthood, an holy nation, a peculiar people; that ye should shew forth the praises of him who hath called you out of darkness into his marvellous light. Which in time past were not a people, but are now the people of God: which had not obtained mercy, but now have obtained mercy."*

Life on the Frontlines, with the persecution of Christians can be very challenging at times. When the bombing of churches by terrorist was daily, believers were praying round the clock.

They had to dig deep into the word of God to find rest and reassurance, but they still had to go to church with danger lurking around them. This is also training in the wild. When family, ministry or work challenges come, the Holy Spirit is there to help believers to soar. You are called and raised to be a sign and a wonder, what others will burn in, you will glow in. The eagle is built in a way that allows it to mount up in the storm.

Paul was an eagle, as a prisoner on a ship, when the storm came and the ship was under attack, he told the way forward. Though a prisoner, he had a relationship with the creator of the universe which put him in command of the ship. The eagle may be alone at 10,000 feet, but he knows he can withstand the storm because of who he is.

**Acts 27:22-27**
*"And now I exhort you to be of good cheer: for there shall be no loss of any man's life among you, but of the ship. For there stood by me this night the angel of God, whose I am, and whom I serve, Saying, Fear not, Paul; thou must be brought before Caesar: and, lo, God hath given thee all them that sail with thee. Wherefore, sirs, be of good cheer: for I believe God, that it shall be*

*even as it was told me. Howbeit we must be cast upon a certain island. But when the fourteenth night was come, as we were driven up and down in Adria, about midnight the shipmen deemed that they drew near to some country."*

Paul knew storms do not destroy eagles. When it was time for Paul, he said, The Lord had shown him, his departure. Jesus laid down his life, it was not snatched away. God did not make a third world Christian, he made a new creation.

We all look the same on the inside, what he does in a believer somewhere else in the world, he would do for another. On the inside of the eagle, it is a warrior, a fighter, a champion. When challenges come, it is an opportunity to look to the God on the inside of the believer.

**Ephesians 1:22-23**
*"And hath put all things under his feet, and gave him to be the head over all things to the church, Which is his body, the fulness of him that filleth all in all. "*

**Ephesians 2:10**
*"For we are his workmanship, created in Christ Jesus unto good works, which God hath before ordained that we should walk in them."*

**1 John 3:8**
*"He that committeth sin is of the devil; for the devil sinneth from the beginning. For this purpose the Son of God was manifested, that he might destroy the works of the devil."*

CATCHING THE CURRENT OF THE SPIRIT

The eagle lives by revelation. It waits and catches the right current. She has microscopic and telescopic eyesight, she can see near and far, her sight is very keen. A believer must live by the revealed word of God. There are things you will know in your spirit because of the Holy Spirit within you. You are able to tap into the knowledge of God and you are an oddity in the world. They don't understand how you navigate, how you are kept from danger. It is the spirit of God that does this.

The eagle is known to perch for days waiting on the right current, once she latches on to this current she can ride it to her destination. A believer can learn through personal intimacy to discern the current of the Holy Spirit.

Those who crucified Jesus were of the opinion that they had successfully terminated God's agenda, even Satan thought the same. Little did Satan realize that Jesus was the substitute submitted as a lamb to die on the cross for sins, to gain access to hell and defeat him on his own turf, in order that he may take the key of authority and raise believers together with him.

## John 3:8

*"The wind bloweth where it listeth, and thou hearest the sound thereof, but canst not tell whence it cometh, and whither it goeth: so is every one that is born of the Spirit."*

## 1Cor. 2:9 -12

*"But as it is written, Eye hath not seen, nor ear heard, neither have entered into the heart of man, the things which God hath prepared for them that love him. But God hath revealed them unto us by his Spirit: for the Spirit searcheth all things, yea, the deep things of God. For what man knoweth the things of a man, save the spirit of man which is in him? even so the things of God knoweth no man, but the Spirit of God. Now we have received, not the spirit of the world, but the spirit which is of God; that we might know the things that are freely given to us of God."*

Your life is a coded book with access only through the Holy Spirit. Satan throws many things at the church but God uses them as stepping stones for spiritual advancement and training for the next level. It is important to be led by the Holy Spirit.

The more time you spend reading the word, praying in the Holy Spirit, obeying quickly the leadings of the Holy Spirit; the more dynamic and supernatural your life will be.

A revelation generally speaking is information gathered outside your natural senses. It may sound like you, but it is not something that was your mind. Your spirit can release supernatural thought into your mind.

It would be peaceful, biblical, full of love. You need to start with simple things like when your heart smites you and you need to apologize, then do it. When a thought comes suddenly about praying for someone, giving to someone, helping out. Those are God moments that can help to sharpen your Spirit.

Be quiet after praying in tongues, watch out for Bible verses that come to you, divine thoughts and ideas, images of events, where you need to make correction and apologize or repent.

The Holy Spirit will not come down the road wearing a red jacket and ringing a bell. He will not come with loud speakers and a microphone shouting your name because He lives within you. He will pass information through your spirit and your mind will be enlightened.

If you want to know the direction of the wind, pay attention to the leaves, if the buildings are moving you may be too late. Those gentle nudges, lack of peace, restlessness, bubbling joy and peace inside are pointers to the direction to go. You can know a yes or a no in every situation in life.

RENEWAL

The believer needs a season of fasting and isolation where there is communion, renewal and rejuvenation. The oil needs to be renewed. The early church was baptized in the Holy Spirit, but often times we read that they were filled with the Holy Spirit. At such times they have been engaged in a time of prayer, there is one baptism and many fillings.

**Isa 40:28 -31**

*"Hast thou not known? Hast thou not heard, that the everlasting God, the LORD, the Creator of the ends of the earth, fainteth not, neither is weary? There is no searching of his understanding. He giveth power to the faint; and to them that have no might he increaseth strength. Even the youths shall faint and be weary, and the young men shall utterly fall: But they that wait upon the LORD shall renew their*

*strength; they shall mount up with wings as eagles; they shall run, and not be weary; and they shall walk, and not faint."*

**Rom 8:19**

*"For the earnest expectation of the creature waiteth for the manifestation of the sons of God."*

As believers wait on the Lord, there is a renewal or exchange of strength. Believers can exchange their weaknesses for the strength of God. It is in the time of distress that manifests his glory.

All the heroes and heroines of faith in Hebrews 11 were people who rose above challenges that were meant to destroy them. Daniel slept in a lion's den, the three Hebrew children walked in the midst of a fiery furnace, Abraham left his country to wander in a foreign land, Joseph left home with no forwarding address, Paul was either having a revival or in prison, Peter slept the night before his crucifixion and the list goes on.

The challenging season is when God wants to show case to the world His glory in the church.

## A SHAKING IS A TIME OF MANIFESTATION

God is eager to see the church walk in the demonstration of his power and glory. When there are shakings, just like the Eagle, the church is expected to mount up with wings and ride the storm. Our ability to ride the storm depends on how well we have prepared.

The Eagle is the believer ideally considered. We are expected to ride the storm because we are designed to be over-comers. If the believer becomes weary, it is time to come away, spend time in fellowship with the Father; through the word, prayer, fasting, and worship

# BIBLIOGRAPHY

1.     Merriam-Webster.    Dictionary    by Merriam-Webster: America's most-trusted online   dictionary   [cited   2020   Jun   24]. Available   from:   https://www.merriam-webster.com/

2.  Strong J. The Exhaustive Concordance of the Bible. Cincinnati: Jennings & Graham; 1890   [cited   2020   Jun   24].   Available from:https://archive.org/stream/exhausti veconcor1890stro#page/n11/mode/2up

3.   Quote by Smith Wigglesworth: "Great faith is the product of great fights. [cited 2020   Jun   24].   Available   from: https://www.goodreads.com/quotes/6215 74-great-faith-is-the-product-of-great-fights-great-testimonies

# SOME OTHER BOOKS BY DR TUNDE BOLANTA

1) Answering the Call to the Ministry (available In Danish )
2) Insecurity in Ministry
3) Communion and the New Covenant
4) Fear Not
5) Everyday Promises of Jesus
6) Anointing for Endurance
7) Flies in the Ointment
8) Discerning Ditches in the Last Days
9) Seven Benefits of Righteousness
10) Vessel unto Honour
11) Sex Fantasy and Reality
12) Absent Without Leave
13) Mentoring in Life & Ministry
14) Understanding Seasons in Life & Ministry.
15) Spiritual Brokenness (also available in Danish)
16) Tithing Under Grace

17) The Power in the Blood of Jesus
18) Strength for Today (Daily Devotional
    Tina & Tunde Bolanta
19) Faith under Fire

*The Shaking and The Glory*

www.ingramcontent.com/pod-product-compliance
Lightning Source LLC
Chambersburg PA
CBHW022103280326
41933CB00007B/239